AF794598

BEYOND RESULTS: ACCOUNTABILITY, DISCRETION AND PERFORMANCE BUDGET REFORM

CONTEMPORARY STUDIES IN APPLIED BEHAVIORAL SCIENCE

Series Editor: Ron Perry

Recent volumes:

Volume 9:	Some Buildings Just Can't Dance
Volume 10:	A Matter of Ethics: Facing the Fear of Doing the Right Thing

CONTEMPORARY STUDIES IN APPLIED BEHAVIORAL SCIENCE VOLUME 11

BEYOND RESULTS: ACCOUNTABILITY, DISCRETION AND PERFORMANCE BUDGET REFORM

BY

KATHLEEN K. ANDERS
Arizona State University, USA

Emerald

United Kingdom – North America – Japan
India – Malaysia – China

Emerald Group Publishing Limited
Howard House, Wagon Lane, Bingley BD16 1WA, UK

Copyright © 2001 Emerald Group Publishing Limited

Reprints and permission service
Contact: booksandseries@emeraldinsight.com

No part of this book may be reproduced, stored in a retrieval system, transmitted in any form or by any means electronic, mechanical, photocopying, recording or otherwise without either the prior written permission of the publisher or a licence permitting restricted copying issued in the UK by The Copyright Licensing Agency and in the USA by The Copyright Clearance Center. No responsibility is accepted for the accuracy of information contained in the text, illustrations or advertisements. The opinions expressed in these chapters are not necessarily those of the Editor or the publisher.

British Library Cataloguing in Publication Data
A catalogue record for this book is available from the British Library

ISBN: 978-0-76-230744-9

Printed and bound by CPI Group (UK) Ltd, Croydon, CR0 4YY

Awarded in recognition of Emerald's production department's adherence to quality systems and processes when preparing scholarly journals for print

INVESTOR IN PEOPLE

DEDICATED TO
GARY, MARY and TOM

CONTENTS

LIST OF TABLES

LIST OF FIGURES

PREFACE

Holding government accountable for results is the dominant theme in reforming public budgeting today. Efforts to link performance measures to the budget have been an integral part of budget reform for decades. Yet, these earlier attempts (that most agree were not too successful) have done little to dampen the enthusiasm for the current initiative. From a handful of mostly state programs prior to 1990, performance-based budgeting has spread to nearly all the American states, many local governments, and special use districts. It has been adopted by a host of nations including our federal government.

The reasons why performance-based budgeting has been such a fast diffusing reform are many and volumes have been written about its advantages for improving budgetary decision making. One of the most highly touted is its promise to shift the focus in budgeting from controlling costs to purchasing program outcomes. Rules and regulations will be lessened, administrators will be delegated greater discretion, the budget process will be streamlined and government will move "from red tape to results".

This book examines that premise, not with the intent to disparage the idea. It seems a very good one. Yet, it is one thing to argue that administrators should be freed from red-tape and rule-bound processes. It is quite another to make that happen. Practitioners who have been involved in budget reforms (and I number among them) know how difficult and frustrating the process can be. At least part of the reason is that we fail to acknowledge the complexity of implementing change in budgeting and the very real constraints that must be faced in public sector organizations. To understand these constraints it is especially important to place performance budget reform and its hoped-for increase in administrative discretion into a larger framework of public sector accountability.

This study does that by testing the fit between reform expectations and reform outcomes as viewed by practitioners. The theoretical bases for questioning the expectations of reform are grounded in the literature of accountability and budgeting. However, this book is not written just for the academician or budgeting professional. It is also directed toward the public administrator, who may not understand much about budget theory, but who would like to know more about this reform which he or she may now be implementing and, who might also want to learn more about the reasons why performance budget reform may *not* realize change as prescribed.

My research for this book began in 1992 when my own state passed legislation to adopt performance-based budgeting. I thought then, and still think, reformers exaggerate the ability to improve public budgeting by changing the content and structure of the budget information presented to decision makers. Over the past eight years, I've studied budget reform and learned more about performance-based budgeting. Much of my education has been from practitioners across the states involved in reform initiatives. These individuals are far too many to acknowledge here but deserve thanks for the interest they showed in this study and for their generosity in sharing their time, knowledge and ideas on budget reform.

I also wish to thank my teacher, Dr. N. Joseph Cayer, whose careful review of early drafts of the manuscript and constant support over many years was of great help to me in completing this study. I am also most grateful to Dr. Ronald W. Perry. No author could ask for a better, more understanding and supportive editor. Without his patient and expert guidance, I am certain this project would never have been completed.

I. INTRODUCTION

Is there is evidence that performance budget reform, as implemented in the American states, increases the discretion of administrators affording them greater flexibility with which to achieve program goals? While there exists a large body of literature outlining prescriptions for change and why these changes are needed, there has been little investigation into the efficacy of performance budget reform to bring about the outcomes envisioned.

In the United States, and in nations around the world, elected officials and public managers are dealing with low levels of public trust, fiscal constraints, and citizen demands for greater accountability in government (Heeks, 1999; Kettl, 2000; National Performance Review, 1993a; Organization for Economic Cooperation and Development [OECD], 1994, 1995, 1997; Popovich, 1998). A central component of global efforts to address these problems is performance-based budgeting or budgeting for results. This budget reform is "centered around accountability frameworks in which the government entrusts spending agencies with flexibility in using resources, in exchange for holding them responsible for results" (OECD, 1997, p. 12).

Although there are a number of expected outcomes from this initiative that could be examined, the literature on accountability and budgeting suggests that performance budget reform's presumption of increased administrative discretion in return for holding administrators accountable for results especially merits review.

The reporting of performance measures and standards in budgeting is expected to strengthen accountability for results, at the same time lessening the need for ex ante controls and compliance with top-down rules. Reduction in rules, procedures, and reporting requirements is anticipated to provide greater

Beyond Results: Accountability, Discretion and Performance Budget Reform, Volume 11, pages 1–157.
Copyright © 2001 by Elsevier Science Inc.
All rights of reproduction in any form reserved.
ISBN: 0-7623-0744-7

discretion, streamlining the budget process and allowing administrators to better utilize their expertise and knowledge of program needs in budget decisions. But does this in fact happen?

This study surveys administrators and central budget staff across all of the states in the program areas of Corrections, Education K-12, and Revenue. Their assessment of performance budget reform and its relationship to accountability and discretion provide data to empirically test the fit between reform expectations and reform outcomes as perceived by practitioners. It is expected that performance-based budgeting may not realize change as predicted by its advocates because this theory of reform does not sufficiently consider the organizational realities of public administrators today; that is, an environment characterized by multiple and often conflicting accountability claims.

BACKGROUND

Beginning in the 1980s and continuing through today, the focus in public budgeting has been on performance or budgeting for results. This reform is one of a number of initiatives aimed at improving public administration by moving away from an emphasis on compliance with rules and regulations toward holding agencies more accountable for program outcomes.

In performance budgeting, as well as in other prescriptions for reform (e.g. reinventing, deregulating, and minimizing government), a common theoretical assumption is that burdensome, top-down bureaucratic controls must be lessened if public administrators are to become more responsive to both citizens' needs and our fast changing environment. Although improvement in performance has become imperative under conditions of resource scarcity, advocates of reform underplay the difficulty of moving away from a traditional, rule-bound system of accountability toward a system that focuses on results.

In public budgeting, performance initiatives are not new. Federal, state, and local governments have had experience with some form of planning, programming and budgeting systems (PPBS) or with other systems that tried to link budgeting and performance (e.g. zero based budgeting [ZBB] and management by objectives [MBO]). What is distinctive about the current reform is that in exchange for obtaining greater discretion over budgeted resources, administrators commit themselves to specific outputs to result from the implementation of their budgets, and in the ideal case, to the results or outcomes ensuing from these outputs. The objective is for these performance outcomes instead of resource inputs to be the central feature of budget requests.

Clearly, a shift in the emphasis of budgeting from controlling the costs of programs to funding program performance makes sense, and there is a large body of literature on performance budgeting saying just that. In this regard, today's reform is similar to earlier initiatives; that is, the discussion is largely normative, the reform is executive centered, and it promises to change budgeting by improving the information given to decision makers.

What makes less sense, is that this reform initiative has advanced with few questioning how realistic the assumptions are. This is surprising in light of the fact that as a group, budget reforms have not produced striking successes nor have they resulted in the wholesale changes that each promised when enacted. Today's reform with its presumption of increased administrative discretion in return for holding administrators accountable for results is especially questionable.

For at least thirty years, the budgeting literature has criticized reform initiatives for failure to recognize the politics of budgeting. Current literature on budget theory continues to underscore how administrators are subject to elected officials and the politics of the budget process. However, other constraints to budgetary discretion are now discussed. Expenditure limits, mandates from other levels of government and the courts, earmarked revenues, formula funding, multiyear spending commitments, and the vulnerability of the budget to economic conditions suggest that many factors limiting administrative discretion in public budgeting are outside the scope of performance budget reform.

The literature on accountability offers further support for questioning the assumption that performance budget reform will bring about an increase in administrative discretion. It points out the inherent tension between increasing administrative discretion as a means to advance public sector performance while ensuring that waste, abuse, and fraud are protected against. This literature also makes explicit the alternative accountability demands which public administrators are subject to in our democratic system of government and which limit their actions.

A reform that proposes to reorient budgeting from compliance to performance by freeing administrators from ex ante controls while demanding more accountability for results is a fundamental change from the traditional budgeting process. The normative underpinnings of this reform are aimed, as in the past, at making the budget process more rational. Yet, that message has been delivered time and again. Prior experience with budget reforms as well as the literature of budget theory and accountability suggest that the assumptions of this normative model warrant further study.

FOCUS OF THE RESEARCH

Central to this study is the question: Does performance budget reform bring about an increase in administrative discretion? That is, to what extent are current expectations about the benefits of performance budget reform valid? It is proposed that performance budget reform may not realize change in the manner prescriptive theory envisions to the extent that: (1) reform does not bring about expected changes in bureaucratic and political accountability demands, and (2) legal accountability claims and fiscal constraints, which are beyond the scope of this reform, affect administrative discretion in budgeting.

To test these hypotheses, the study employs a cross-sectional design conducted in two phases. All fifty state executive budget offices were first surveyed to determine the status of performance budget reform initiatives as of July, 1996. A nationwide survey of administrators and central budget staff in the program areas of Corrections, Education K-12, and Revenue was then conducted to examine practitioners' views on administrative discretion and whether it increases with the adoption of performance budgeting. Examined are their perceptions regarding the implementation of reform in their state as well as on alternative accountability claims that are expected to affect the efficacy of this reform to influence budget decision making.

Whereas the first area of inquiry emphasizes questions related to how performance budget reform is administered, the second area of inquiry explores the broader question: To whom and for what are public administrators accountable? Surprisingly, this question has received little attention by reform advocates even though redirecting accountability from compliance with rules toward a focus on results assumes a change in what administrators are accountable for that is supported by entities with oversight authority.

In budgeting, public administrators are accountable to multiple and overlapping authorities (e.g. elected officials and political appointees, the courts, and other levels of government). Associated with these actors are different mechanisms for ensuring accountability and different views as to what accountability means. This inquiry is intended to make explicit these alternative accountability claims viewed in terms of how practitioners perceive that administrative discretion is influenced by political, legal, and bureaucratic accountability demands as well as fiscal constraints that typify today's budgeting environment.

The contemporary literature in budget theory suggests that public sector reformers may exaggerate the ability to control expenditures. A central premise is that much of what occurs in budgeting can be traced to the need of decision makers to deal with situations that frequently involve diverse and external constraints. This study is designed to examine the constraints to discretion that practitioners face and for this reason individuals – agency administrators and central budget staff – are the unit of analysis.

By seeking responses from two different groups a more impartial assessment of performance budget reform may be gained than would be found from a single perspective, such as central budget analysts whose role may be organizational advocates for change or agency administrators whose commitments to existing programs may cause them to feel threatened by the change of reform. Also, the two perspectives offer different frames of reference. Agency administrators are especially knowledgeable of program activities, clients, statutory mandates and other programmatic information which may affect discretion. However, central budget offices typically engage in revenue forecasting activities, oversight and management of spending across all programs of state government, affording analysts a better understanding of external political and fiscal constraints.

Both respondent groups in the program areas of Education K-12, Corrections, and Revenue are surveyed. Because of the proportion of resources allocated to education and its perceived importance to citizens and elected officials, Education K-12 was among the first program areas focused on for the application of performance measures (Government Accounting Standards Board [GASB], 1990). Corrections is today, one of the fast growing areas in state spending. Revenue departments serve key functions in state government particularly with respect to public budgeting and finance. Also, these areas were selected because they are consistent across all state government budget offices and represent very different program areas. By examining responses grouped by program areas, some which may be more subject to external controls than others (e.g. corrections by the courts), it may also be possible to capture some of the differences across programs with respect to accountability, discretion, and reform.

Because the study is designed to identify disparities between what we expect from performance budget reform and what practitioners perceive to be its effects, the prescriptions of performance budget reform frame the inquiry. The focus of the research is not directed toward criticizing performance budgeting initiatives, but toward bringing practitioners' perceptions on the implementation of reform into a discussion that has been largely normative. Relative to practice, an objective is to better align the expectations of this reform with administrators' perceptions of their ability to effect change. With respect to theory, an objective is to move beyond the traditional critique of budget reform efforts, the politics of budgeting, by considering alternative accountability claims and constraints that administrators are answerable to and which limit their actions. By making explicit these multiple accountability demands, our understanding of the difficulties practitioners face in realizing the desired changes from this reform may be improved.

SIGNIFICANCE OF THE STUDY

Confronting the difficulties of reforming the budgeting process is a significant contribution to a literature that frequently focuses on proposals for change and on enumerating reasons why policy makers should adopt them. According to Rubin (1990), budget reform proposals have not kept up with the complex reality of budgeting today. The result is "a series of unrelated, and sometimes worn-out proposals, many of which have little potential for success" (p. 187). Bunch and Straussman (1993) think that the new movement in budgetary research and theory has failed to penetrate "the real world" of budgeting (p. 19). They believe that budgeting will be "improved" only if reformers "begin with a perspective on how organizations actually behave rather than how we would like them to act" (p. 29). Premchand (1998) identifies a similar need to move away from "umbrella themes to specifics and details of operation" (p. 87). He argues that, if reforms are to succeed, we must shift attention from broad principles and values of reform toward identifying "the problems that remain to be recognized, fully analyzed and addressed" (p. 74).

On the whole, the literature of budget reform has been comprised of either prescriptions for or descriptions of management innovations. Less attention has been directed to what, in fact, reforms have accomplished. This is in spite of the fact that the history of reform demonstrates nothing so much as the formidable difficulties in translating reform objectives into practical budget routines.

Lack of evidence, however, has seldom diminished the fervor of proponents, nor has it dissuaded practitioners. At the federal level, the movement toward performance budgeting is most visible in the Chief Financial Officers Act of 1990 and the Government Performance and Results Act (GPRA) of 1993. The GPRA, which received overwhelming bipartisian support, requires federal agencies to develop and submit to the Director of the Office of Management and Budget and to Congress five-year strategic plans, one-year performance plans and link performance indicators to budget requests. In addition, performance budget reform is among the recommendations of Vice President Gore's National Performance Review Commission which focuses on correcting a "performance deficit" in federal public service (National Performance Review [NPR], 1993a).

Many state governments have also implemented, to varying degrees, their own versions of GPRA and NPR. The National Association of State Budget

Officers (NASBO) (1997) reports that forty-eight states use performance measurement data in their budget process, an increase of forty-five percent from 1990 (NASBO, 1990, 1997). As part of this study, it was found that forty of the fifty states have an ongoing effort to integrate measures of performance, including outcome measures, into their budget process (Anders, 1996). This is consistent with other recent studies of state budgeting that find at least eighty percent of the states have undertaken efforts to implement performance budget reform (Jordan & Hackbart, 1999; Melkers & Willoughby, 1998; NASBO, 1997). While states adopt different approaches to reform, often using budget guidelines and instructions to implement changes, thirty-one states have codified into law performance-based budgeting requirements (Melkers & Willoughby, 1998).

Among recent developments at the local government level, the Governmental Accounting Standards Board (GASB) (1990, 1992, 1994) has been studying ways for state and local governments to include measures of performance (i.e. service efforts and accomplishments) in their externally reported financial statements. Multigovernment efforts to promote the use of performance measures and reporting in cities and counties are also being advanced by the Urban Institute, the International City/County Management Association (ICMA), as well as by academic institutes such as the Institute of Government, University of North Carolina; the Government Performance Project at the Maxwell School, Syracuse University, and the National Center for Public Productivity, at Rutgers University (Coe, 1999; ICMA, 1999, Hatry, 1999; Kopcynski & Lombardo, 1999).

Given such a high level of interest in this reform initiative and large numbers of performance budgeting systems under development in the United States as well as abroad, this research is timely, useful and worthy of attention. Furthermore, several specific factors can be mentioned to support the significance of this study.

First, the systematic collection of data on the implementation of performance budget reform adds to the knowledge about the sophistication of performance budgeting systems in the states. Second, the study examines the normative assumption of a theory of budget reform. It elicits practitioners' perceptions concerning administrative discretion and whether it increases with the adoption of performance budgeting, a subject about which little is known. It is conceivable that practitioners may report that performance budget reform enhances their discretion and provides them greater flexibility in budget decision making. This finding would confirm the prescriptive theory of performance budget reform and, while contradicting the hypotheses argued here, it would contribute to our understanding of the relationship between reform and discretion.

However, it is expected that this will not be the finding of this study. To consider the other extreme, practitioners may regard performance budget reform as an added reporting requirement of the existing top-down accountability system. It may be perceived to produce added paperwork in compliance with more bureaucratic controls, diminishing rather than enhancing discretion, in effect, bringing about the opposite of what reform sets out to accomplish. As Wildavsky (1980) put it, "Until we know something about the 'existential situation' in which the participants find themselves, proposals for major reform must be based on woefully inadequate understanding" (p. 78).

Third, since the study examines both agency administrators' and central budget analysts' perceptions of reform, comparison of respondent groups may provide insight into barriers to administrative discretion which may be possible to remedy through changes in how performance budgeting is implemented. Also, information on constraints to discretion compared by program may improve our understanding about the implementation of performance budgeting in different task environments.

Finally, examining performance budget reform in terms of diverse accountability claims introduces an alternative framework for inquiry into budget reform. This framework could provide the foundation for the development of a descriptive theory that better explains the reality practitioners face in advancing reform – one that does not evade the difficult problems of designing change in our democratic system, but instead makes explicit a number of these problems and affords a new basis for inquiry into their solution.

PLAN OF THE BOOK

Chapter I has presented an overview of the book by briefly describing performance budget reform and how the literature of budget theory and accountability raise questions regarding the assumption that administrative discretion will increase with its adoption. The focus of the research, which is primarily designed to examine the relationship between performance budget reform and discretion and how it may be affected by alternative accountability claims, was also described. Finally, the significance of the research was discussed.

Chapter II begins by presenting an overview of the budget process and approaches to its reform. It then examines performance based reforms that were tried in the past and reviews today's initiative as prescribed by its advocates and as discussed in the literature.

In Chapter III the theoretical bases for questioning the expectations of this reform are considered: first, in terms of traditional criticism of budget reform initiatives or the politics of budgeting and second, in terms of new directions in budget theory and alternative conceptions of accountability which describe constraints to discretion that are largely outside the scope of budget reform.

Chapter IV introduces the research methods employed in this study, describes the research questions, and how the principal concepts were measured. The study design section further specifies the data collection strategy and the data analysis approach.

Chapter V presents the profile of the survey respondents and results of the data analyses. The survey results are related to each of the research questions posed by the study and discussed.

Chapter VI interprets the results of the study from the broader perspective of both theory and practice. The implications of the findings for performance budget reform and its promise of increased discretion is considered. It also examines the limitations of the study and suggests possibilities for future related research.

Chapter VII offers concluding remarks and outlines a proposal for rethinking our approach to budget reform in a way that builds on the findings of this study. This discussion presents an alternative framework for understanding how to improve public budgeting, modeling it on a common premise of financial management, and one known to most individuals who invest: a portfolio approach to budget reform.

II. AN OVERVIEW OF BUDGET REFORM

Public administrators in budgeting have long complained that they cannot do their jobs properly because of too much political interference, too little ability to innovate, and too little discretion (National Performance Review, 1993a; Schick, 1966; Wildavsky, 1964, 1992b). Much of the literature of budget theory addresses budget reform and discusses prescriptions for more rational budget processes. This study, which examines whether practice is perceived to be consistent with performance reform prescriptions, draws upon that literature and on the literature of accountability.

This chapter begins by presenting an overview of the budget process and approaches to its reform. It then reviews prior performance-based reforms and examines today's initiative as prescribed in the literature. The problem of how to increase administrative discretion while preserving accountability is then considered in terms of performance budgeting's response, accountability for results.

THE BUDGET PROCESS

"A full explanation of all factors that have a bearing on the budget process", writes Wildavsky (1986), "would exhaust everyone without enlightening anyone. It would look more like a laundry list than a coherent explanation" (p. 3). What is important, he goes on to argue, is knowledge of the more permanent and persistent features of the budget process. Taking a historical and comparative perspective Naomi Caiden (1994) notes that while every jurisdiction is characterized by its own distinctive political and cultural contexts, budgeting itself "the translation of financial resources into human purposes" is ultimately an identical and necessary activity all over the world (p. 44).

At the most parsimonious level, explains Schick (1988), budgeting is a process about claiming and conserving resources. It is not the only means by which money and other resources are claimed. Markets perform these functions. Claims are also made by war and other acts of violence. However, what distinguishes budgeting is that claims are to be made and resources distributed according to rules and procedures.

These rules and procedures can vary greatly dependent upon the legal, political and economic context of the jurisdiction (Bartle, 1999; N. Caiden, 1994; OECD, 1997; Rubin, 1992; Wildavsky, 1986). In the United States, federal, state and local budgeting processes differ in significant ways (Bunch & Straussman, 1993; Clynch & Lauth, 1991; Lynch, 1990). As Axelrod (1988) points out, "the fund structure of the federal government is sheer simplicity compared to the dazzling diversity of funds in state government" (p. 233). These different structures result in a multiplicity of fragmented and cumbersome accounts that complicate the budget process.

Because public budgeting is responsive to social, economic, and political influences, it "is not an isolated practice that operates – or changes— independently of the environment in which it exists" (Schick, 1980, p. 11). The budgeting system, Lewis (2000) observes "adapts in small steps, often seemingly in slow motion, and generally by accretion of new rules, statutes and institutes. The result today is a system that is cumbersome, even byzantine, and beyond facile comprehension" (p. 184).

A common view, shared by those new to the field and budget scholars, is that public budgeting is complex and becoming increasingly more so. Exception can be taken to the very notion of a single budget. There are usually several which can be referred to depending on what one has in mind insofar as the scope and coverage of government activities (e.g. operating budget, capital budget) or the manner in which various items are treated in an accounting sense (e.g. obligational authority, obligations incurred, accrued expenditures). In discussions of the budget process and its reform, it is the executive's administrative budget or set of accounts that receives legislative attention that is commonly referred to as "the budget".

During the first decades of the 1900s, the executive budget was regarded as fundamental to government reform. As Schick (1980) writes:

> Administrative reorganization and the 'budget idea' (as it was called by reformers) were coupled in countless studies into a cohesive statement on the elements of good government. It was generally thought that administrative efficiency and budgeting were interdependent, that one could not be realized without the other. No mayor or governor, the argument ran, could efficiently operate his government without command over the budget process. The National Municipal League's *Model State Constitution* (first issued in 1921) embraced this view by advocating an integrated administrative structure with the governor in charge of preparing and carrying out the state's budget (p. 3).

Since that time, budgeting's role in promoting the value of efficiency in government has endured. Moreover, various administrative and political uses have been added to budgeting to take advantage of its action forcing capacity and its command of the public purse (Schick, 1988; White, 1994). As Osborne and Gaebler (1992) note in their now classic book, *Reinventing Government*: "In government, the most important lever – the system that drives behavior most powerfully – is the budget" (p. 161). A result is that budgeting has become a process in which reformers often concentrate on managerial change with less focus on resource constraints. However, as Rubin (1995) emphasizes "the essence of budgeting is that it allocates scarce resources and hence implies choice between potential objects of expenditure" (p. 2).

It may seem rudimentary, but in discussions of budget reform, including today's initiatives focused on budgeting for results, the concept of resource scarcity is not always acknowledged. Yet, this is among the most permanent features of budgeting and implicit in the very term. That is, claims for resources add up to more than is available and there is a ceiling or a constraint which requires governments to spend within certain limits.

For example, a program may perform very well as evaluated under a performance-based process and achieve all expected results but not be funded in the budget due to the dollars available. Similar observations have been made about earlier reforms such as planning, programming, and budgeting systems (PPBS) that operate "without global spending limits" (Wildvasky, 1992b, p. 438). Wildavsky (1992b) criticized both PPBS and zero-based budgeting (ZBB) as "expressions of a view in which ranking objectives is rendered tantamount to reason. . . . For purposes of resource allocation, which is what budgeting is about, it is irrational to rank objectives without considering resources (pp. 439–440)."

Public budgeting, furthermore, is subject not only to economic constraints, but also to constraints imposed by other levels of government, constitutional and statutory limits and to perceived limits imposed by public opinion (Rubin, 1992, p. 6). As a consequence, budgeting is not only a process that seeks to install economic efficiency in the provisions of government goods and services but also a mechanism for achieving political consensus by reconciling conflicts about who shall pay for and receive budgetary benefits.

Yet, despite the politics and technical complexity, "budgeting is a distinct area, easily recognizable from legislative or executive behavior or politics in general" (Rubin, 1988, p. 6). First, it is a process not an institution. It cuts across institutions. Second, the concreteness of budgeting differentiates it from other political processes (Caiden, 1990; Rubin, 1990; Schick, 1994a; Wildavsky, 1992b). The budget process has fixed deadlines. Government cannot operate without interruption if the budget process does not meet them. Time, therefore, is a crucial factor in terms of the amount of it available in which to analyze decisions as well as in terms of the cumulative effect of past and present decisions on future budget outcomes.

Typically, the time periods at issue are fiscal years. The budget process is described in terms of a cycle which is linked to an annual or biennial fiscal year(s). This cycle consists of a series of events including preparation, revision, adoption, execution and audit (Howard, 1973; Lee & Johnson, 1989; Lynch, 1990).

Budget Cycle

Preparation includes estimates of the upcoming fiscal year's revenues, the establishment of general guidelines by the chief executive and submission by departments of proposed expenditures. Revenue forecasting sets the stage for all future budget deliberations. If a forecast offers the prospect for surplus revenues, the general guidelines and ensuring agency debates are likely to be very different from those that are conducted under conditions of shortfalls (Klay, 1992, p. 211). "At all levels of government", notes Schick (1994b), "gapmanship – closing or narrowing the projected gap between revenues and expenditures dominates the budget preparation process" (p. 4).

Since the U.S. Budget Reconciliation Act of 1921 at both the federal and state government level, revenue forecasting along with the setting of guidelines and formulation of department budgets are the task of the executive. However in the past twenty years, federal and state legislative bodies have increasingly become active participants in revenue estimation and in some cases propose their own budget for agencies (Cogan, Muris & Schick, 1994; Hackbart & Carlson, 1993; Cynch & Lauth, 1991).

Revision and adoption involves consideration of alternative claims for funds and translates the proposed budget plan into policy or law. The central budget office evaluates programs and funding requested by departments. It also is assigned the task of bringing department budgets in line with the priorities of the elected executive and with revenue constraints (Bunch & Straussman, 1993). Paul Appleby (1957) labels the budget office's role as "preponderantly negative" often serving as a countervailing force against the expansionary demands of public agencies (p. 157). Schick (1980) suggests this is the budget office's function "as the institutionalize 'no', resisting the pressures advanced from other quarters" (p. 4).

The executive's proposed budget is then reviewed by the legislature which typically passes the budget bill prior to the beginning of the new fiscal year.

The legislative authorization and appropriation process decides "whose preferences are to prevail in disputes", that is, "who shall receive budgetary benefits and how much" (Wildavsky 1992a, p. 595). This "power of the purse" (Fenno, 1966) gives elected officials strong oversight over departments' budget requests and sets in law which programs are funded. The chief executive is then able to concur, by signing, or reject, by vetoing (in some cases by line-item) appropriated expenditures.

Execution or *implementation* turns budget appropriations into services and is the task of the executive branch. In this phase, the budget is used as guidance for specific decisions by departments. *Audit*, the final phase of the budget process, may range from a focus on the regularity of expenditures (financial audits), to a comprehensive review in which the efficiency and effectiveness of programs are also examined (performance audits). Both serve to hold agencies accountable to a third party and ensure objectivity and fairness in reporting (Greathouse & Funkhouser, 1988).

According to Brown and Pyers (1998), the inclusion of performance measures in the budget makes the audit phase even more important. They argue that "not requiring periodic, systematic audits of such data would be tantamount to requiring the reporting of misleading data" (p. 111). Mosso (1999) too believes the audit is key to an effective performance-based system. Expressing less than positive views of the budget process, he maintains that an independent audit "opens a small window on the world that is relatively unfogged by the gamesmanship that undermines the credibility of financial information emitted by the typical budget process" (p. 73).

While this budget cycle is one of the most common approaches toward understanding the budget process, there is no single such cycle in operation. Rather a cycle exist for each budget period, and several cycles are in operation at any given time. As Bledsoe (1991) points out "budget professionals are often working on three and possibly even four fiscal year budgets at the same time" (p. 31). Preparation may begin a full year or more before the beginning of the budgeted fiscal year. An audit may be completed a year or more after the fiscal year has ended. This results in a significant lag before actual expenditure and revenue data are available. At times, particularly during economic downturns, this can force adjustments midway into the fiscal year further confounding the process (Lee & Johnson, 1989, p. 49; Lynch, 1990, pp. 6–7).

Budget Functions

Related to budget cycles are functions. Axelrod (1988) describes eight interrelated functions which run through every segment of the budget cycle from budget preparation to its audit: (1) Allocating resources to programs designed to achieve governmental priorities; (2) Raising funds through taxes and loans to finance government; (3) Stabilizing the economy through fiscal policies, (primarily a national function); (4) Holding operating agencies accountable for efficient use of resources; (5) Controlling expenditures to make certain they are legal and comply with the policies of political decision makers; (6) Providing a mechanism for transferring funds from one level of government to another; (7) Serving as a mechanism for achieving planned social and economic change and (8) Providing leverage through the power of the purse to improve agency management of programs.

Schick's (1966, 1990) model of the budget process narrows these functions to three: control, management, and planning. Drawing, in part, from the earlier work of Robert Anthony (1965), he argues that the budget process is used to insure legal compliance and to hold down spending (control), as a tool for efficient delivery of services (management), and as a mechanism for setting goals and analyzing alternative courses of action (planning).

Schick maintains that budget processes evolve over time, that is, through stages of budget development from control – strict accounting of expenditures; to management – attention to work efficiency; to planning – consideration of program effectiveness. For Schick, successful control mechanisms are essential to basic budgetary development. These involve the establishment of strong internal accounting systems assuring that specific tasks are carried out. Management functions are added to the control functions to ensure operational efficiency and the accomplishment of organizational objectives. Planning further establishes budgeting processes that stress objectives and the analysis of alternative actions.

While elements of each function are present in all budget types, one will typically predominate in the operation of any single system. A basic theme in approaching the budget process in terms of functions, is that better budgeting can be obtained by advancing the orientation of the process from control to management and planning.

Budget Process Reform

Schick's (1966) classifications of the budget process embracing elements of control, management, and planning has often been used to structure review of reforms (Gray, Jenkins & Segsworth, 1993; Ervin, 1980; Grizzle, 1986; Lee & Johnson, 1989; Stanford, 1990). Under this framework, each function is expressed in a specific budgetary form developing from a simple line item arrangement to more sophisticated formats. Budget reforms are presumed to progress historically from an immature to a mature budget process in which first control, then management, and finally all three functions are firmly embedded.

It should be pointed out, however, that there are other types of initiatives to reform budgeting. At the federal level, the balanced budget amendment illustrated the loss of confidence in political budgetary decision making. The presidential line-item veto is a reform proposal to alter budgetary roles and increase the power of the executive. Performance-based budgeting, similar to Schick's typology, introduces a new budget format to the budget process with the expectation that changing the content and structure of the formal information presented to decision makers will change budgetary outcomes.

In this study, budget process reform assumes the last meaning which is not uncommon though seldom is it explicitly differentiated from the others. Changing budgetary roles as a means to reform the budget process is representative of one of the earliest and most enduring budget reforms – the executive's role in preparing the budget. This is often the emphasis in political science literature. However, examining shifts in the balance of influence between the executive and legislative branches is not the focus here.

A balanced budget amendment is not a budget process reform as much as it is a further attempt to do by law what once was done through the budget process – control spending (McIntyre, 1980, p. 60). Whether or how this type of reform improves budgeting is also not addressed except to point out its underlying assumption is present in many dimensions (i.e. tax and expenditure limitations). That is, the belief that the way to bring fiscal discipline to the budget process is to limit the monies available.

PERFORMANCE-BASED REFORMS

Performance based reforms are founded upon the principle that changing the format and information presented in the budget process will improve budgeting. Specifically, information assessing how well government performs in delivering goods and services will enhance budgetary decision making. In general, "performance budgeting" has been described as "the process of linking expected results to budget levels" (U.S. General Accounting Office [GAO], 1997, p. 1). While this approach to budgeting has garnered considerable attention in recent years, the concept is not new. It was first recommended for use in the federal government by the Hoover Commission in 1949 and considered by the International City Management Association as early as 1938.

Dissatisfied with the traditional line-item or "object" budget for its inability to link public expenditures to public accomplishments, the Hoover Commission recommended enactment of "performance budgets". The Commission believed that performance budgets "would focus attention upon the general character and relative importance of the work to be done, or upon the service to be rendered, rather than upon the things to be acquired . . . [which] are, after all, only the means to an end" (Commission on the Organization of the Executive Branch of the Government, 1949, p. 8).

Under performance budgeting outlined by the Commission, budget categories were to be organized in functional terms and appropriations made to program activities rather than line items. The concept of operational analysis was also introduced and methods were established to measure inputs (i.e. personal services) against outputs and how many units of activity occurred as a result (Hatry, 1989). This first use of the budget as a tool in quantifying performance was followed in the 1950s and 1960s by *program budgeting and planning, programming, budgeting systems (PPBS).*

Program budgeting and PPBS organized budget expenditures around program functional activities and measured efficiency, like performance budgeting, but also emphasized a linkage to program objectives and planning. The basic idea underlying program budgeting and PPBS was that budgetary decisions should be based on output categories (e.g. objectives and end products) rather than simply inputs (e.g. personnel and equipment costs) (Downs & Larkey, 1986, p. 151; Pilegge, 1992, p. 75)

Program budgeting begins with the identification of program goals. "Programs", the primary budget categories, are established by grouping activities that contribute to the same objective which may or may not follow the organizational structure of the government entity. Instead of administrative units, the end products of expenditures and services are the focus of attention. The budget process funds those tasks that contribute to achievement of program objectives. By allocating resources to the most efficient and effective means for achieving ends, performance is to be improved (Axelrod, 1989; Schick, 1966).

In the 1960s wider acceptance of Keynesian economic principles, which emphasized government planned spending as an impetus to economic growth, plus new information and decision technologies, gave rise to PPBS. Originating in the Department of Defense, it was introduced to other departments and agencies of the federal government during the Johnson administration. Charles Hitch, former comptroller of the Defense Department and the man usually credited with installing PPBS there, described it as combining program forecasting and systems analysis. Program forecasting focuses on program goals rather than on expenditures and on projecting both inputs and outputs into the future. Systems analysis seeks to apply quantitative methods to compare alternative courses of action (Downs & Larkey, 1986, p. 151; Pilegge, 1992, p. 75).

Under this budget system, *planning* establishes the goals of the organization and the selection of programs best able to achieve these goals. *Programming* entails the efficient timing and management of tasks, and when necessary sub-tasks, that lead to achievement of each program objective. Lastly, *budgeting* converts goals, programs and tasks into resource estimates. Under PPBS budgeting became one component of a rationally planned iterative process. There was to be continuous re-examination of program results in relationship to anticipated costs and outcomes. These in turn would determine need for changes in programs and objectives as originally established (Miller, 1992; Schick, 1966, 1973).

PPBS was followed by *management by objectives (MBO)* which was introduced in the federal government by the Nixon administration in the early 1970s. MBO originated as a business management technique and had been adopted on a widespread basis in the private sector after it became popularized in the writings of Peter Drucker (1954, 1964).

Like PPBS, management by objectives relied upon the ability to clearly define goals and objectives. Similar to performance budgeting, it demanded an ability to measure performance against specific, quantifiable standards. However, unlike PPBS, MBO emphasized primarily managerial aspects of budget implementation and was not an alternative system for budget preparation. Instead, the focus was on selecting targets and the resources needed to meet them, with benchmarks along the way to measure performance and provide feedback for both personnel appraisal and planning for the next budget cycle. In this regard, MBO offered a more participative approach with program managers heavily involved in setting their own budget targets (Rose, 1977).

Zero-base budgeting (ZBB) requires budgeters to evaluate all programs and activities and to appraise performance as well as cost. In 1970, no state was known to be using ZBB techniques, though by the end of the decade nearly half the states and the federal government had adopted the process (Schick, 1979, p. 1). It was brought to national attention in the writings of Pyhrr (1977), who developed ZBB for Texas Instruments Corporation; however, the idea was advanced as early as 1952 by Verne Lewis.

Lewis's approach was to think in terms of "alternative budgeting" that is, to weigh the consequences of allocating funds for one project and not for another. Zero-base budgeting, in concept, attempts to systematize the weighing of budget alternatives by clarifying the substance of various options and determining the priority of possible allocations. In its pure form, ZBB requires a priority ranking of all programs and activities in successively increasing levels of performance and funding, starting from zero (Phyrr, 1977; Schick, 1979).

Under ZBB, activities are grouped in "decision packages" which are systematically analyzed and ranked in order of importance. Ultimately, each activity contained in the package is to be considered in terms of reduced, current and increased levels of effort and funding. In this way, managers present higher-level decision makers with several choices to select from, rather than a single set of recommended figures. The costs and benefits of alternative packages would be considered, and theoretically the most effective in terms of return is chosen.

BUDGETING FOR RESULTS

Today's "performance budgeting", sometimes referred to as "budgeting for results" (OECD, 1994, 1995; Schick, 1990), aims, as did reforms in the past, at shifting the focus in budgeting from items of government spending to the performance of its programs. Yet, the current reform is distinguished from prior initiatives by: (1) a focus on measures of results or outcomes of performance linked to a strategic planning process; (2) an emphasis on decentralizing control and cutting red tape in budgetary decision making and, (3) a shift in accountability from compliance with rules toward responsibility for results.

Performance Measurement

In performance budgeting of the 1950s, the principal aim of performance measurement was toward helping administrators assess the work of operating units by determining unit cost data, workload measurements and relative measures of efficiency (Miller, 1992; Pilegge, 1992). Under today's reform, performance measures are considered not only as an assessment of efficiency in the execution of the budget, but also as a basis for budget preparation (NASBO, 1995), authorization (National Conference of State Legislatures [NCSL], 1994) and audit (Apostolou, Brooks & Hildreth, 1992; Brown & Pyers, 1998; Buschor & Schedler, 1994; GASB, 1990, 1992, 1994; Gray, Jenkins & Segsworth, 1993; Harris, 1995; Mosso, 1999; Sandberg, 1996; Wheat, 1991).

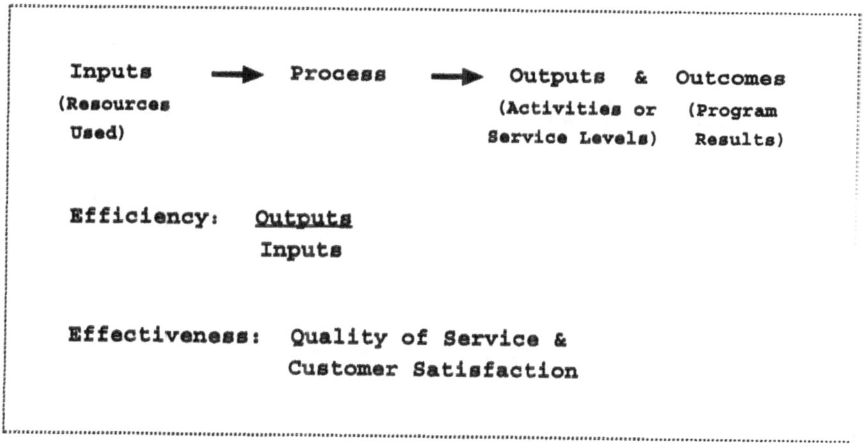

Fig. 1. Types of Performance Measures.

A *performance measure* is defined as "a quantitative or qualitative characterization of performance" (National Performance Review [NPR], 1997, p.6), *performance measurement* is:

> A process of assessing progress towards achieving predetermined goals, including information on the efficiency with which resources are transformed into goods and services (outputs), the quality of those outputs (how well they are delivered to clients and to the extent to which clients are satisfied) and outcomes (the results of a program activity compared to its intended purpose), and the effectiveness of government operations in terms of their specific contributions to program objectives (Ibid., p. 6).

As suggested by NPR, there is a distinct vocabulary used to discuss performance measures. The most commonly set of terms adopted by federal, state, and local governments are shown in Fig. 1 (ICMA, 1999; Leithe, 1997; NPR, 1997).

Under performance-based budgeting, instead of the traditional focus on administrative units and objects-of-expenditure, the program and its end products (e.g. outcomes and outputs) are to be the focus of funding. "Programs", the primary budget categories, are established by grouping activities that contribute to the same objective which may or may not follow the organizational structure of the agency or department.

As illustrated by the examples of measures in Fig. 2, program outcomes are expected to reflect the impact or public benefit of an organization's actions whereas outputs measure the quantity of goods or services produced. Efficiency measures indicate the inputs used to produce an activity, service level or result

INPUTS	**Dollars**	**Number of Full Time Employees**	**Labor Hours**
OUTPUTS	**Number of clients served**	**Number of interviews conducted**	**Number of applications processed**
EFFICIENCY	**Cost: Average cost per client served**	**Productivity: Number of clients per case worker**	**Timeliness: Average time to process applications**
OUTCOMES	**Percentage of population served**	**Percentage of clients satisfied with service**	**Percentage of applications approved within 48 hrs with less than 3% error rate**

Fig. 2. Examples of Performance Measures By Type.

and provide information about production at a given level of resource use (Dupont-Morales & Harris, 1994, p. 231).

Each type of measure can provide a basis for comparing the performance of the budget unit with past performance, internally established levels or performance targets, generally accepted norms or standards, results achieved by similar organizations, or the best organization (Epstein, 1992, 1996; Grifel, 1993; Wholey & Hatry, 1992).

"Benchmark" is often used synonymously with these comparisons, but this term can connote different meanings. Benchmarks have been referred to as a standard, best practice, or performance level targeted by the budget unit. "Benchmarking", first used in the private sector, refers to the process of seeking the best practice and attempting to emulate it. Benchmarking is also practiced in the public sector but it may be more loosely applied to mean any comparisons of performance (ICMA, 1997).

Other terms that are used in conjunction with performance reporting are "service efforts and accomplishments" coined by the Governmental Accounting Standards Board (GASB) (1990, 1992, 1994). The GASB, which sets standards for state and local financial reporting, has taken steps toward requiring these governments to adopt "service efforts and accomplishments" in which measures of performance, or accomplishments, are linked to the budget in externally reported financial statements. GASB does recommend that governments use standard indicators of performance (i.e. inputs, outputs, outcome, and efficiency measures) but labels inputs as "service efforts", outputs and outcomes as "service accomplishments" and efficiency measures as "indicators that relate service efforts to service accomplishments".

GASB also endorses the use of "explanatory information". This would be information, quantitative or descriptive, that can help the reader better understand the measures and the significance of any underlying factors that may have affected the reported performance. Environmental and demographic characteristics, such as weather conditions and population growth rates, would be two examples.

Strategic Planning and Performance Measures

A principal purpose of performance measurement is to assess a budget unit's progress toward strategic program outcomes. By emphasizing program outcomes rather than just outputs or dollar inputs, performance-based budgeting is to bring about budgetary decisions that reflect spending priorities and expectations of program results (NCSL, 1994). However, before performance outcomes can be integrated into the budget process in a meaningful way, agreement must be reached on program goals and priorities.

Like prior reforms, performance-based budgeting emphasizes planning as outlined under PPBS, and achieving goals as targeted under MBO. However, the goals identified and measured under performance-based budgeting are not just short term objectives as focused on under MBO but longer term, strategic objectives. Planning too moves beyond forecasting costs and benefits of alternative program choices. Instead, budgeting is linked to a larger strategic planning process that extends beyond a single annual/biennial budget cycle.

Some benefits that can be expected from integrating strategic planning and budgeting are: (1) improved continuity and reduced uncertainty through the establishment of clear expectations for an agency; (2) improved information for the legislature and public; (3) more effective resource allocation based on the identification of critical issues documented by performance indicators; and (4) stronger linkages between planning, budgeting and evaluation which improve the provision of government programs and services (National Association of State Budget Officers, 1996).

These benefits are enhanced by ensuring that measures used at different levels of government are aligned and consistent. As shown in Fig. 3, goals and performance measures may be desegregated and linkages made to higher order

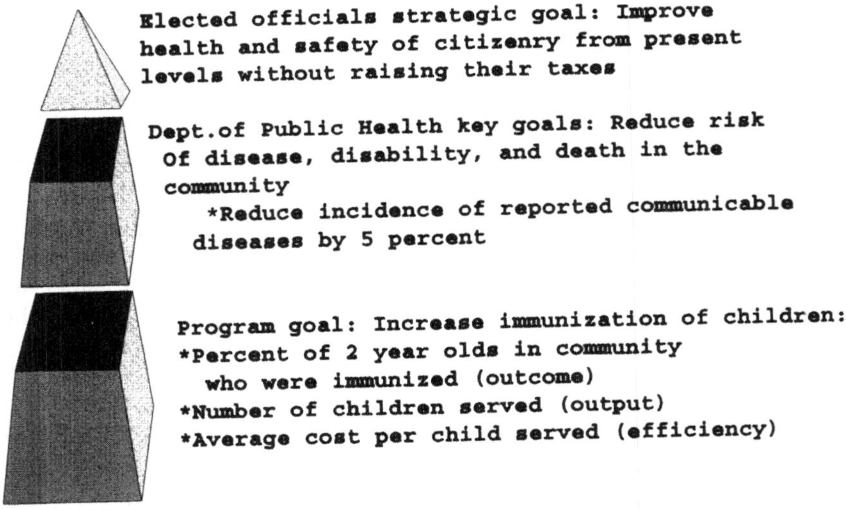

Fig. 3. Alignment of Strategic Goals and Measures.

measures, developing a hierarchy of goals that cascade throughout the government (CFO Council, 1997, p. 1–7; Franklin, 1999, p. 204–205). Aligning measures in this way acknowledges the potential for multiple uses of performance information by different actors whose interest in the information are at different levels of aggregation. Emphasizing the link between elected officials' and administrators' goals also addresses past reforms' failures to connect the planning and goal setting process in the executive and legislative branches (GAO, 1997). It furthermore provides a framework within the bureaucracy for senior officials to better understand the purposes and functions of programs they administer as well as for program managers to understand the importance of their own efforts.

Relative to the selection of measures, as shown in Fig. 3, a balance of output, outcome, and efficiency measures should be reported to fully understand their meaning. While program outcomes are the emphasis in today's reform, other types of measures are needed to provide information on the context of results. For instance, as illustrated, achieving a 2% increase in the number of children immunized can be better understood if the dollar cost per child is for an increase of 2% of 10,000 or 200 children versus 2% of 1,000 or 20 more children served.

Overall, it is recommended that performance measures and performance measurement systems be developed using the following criteria :

- *Appropriateness and Validity.* Does the measure relate to the government objectives for that service and does it really measure the degree to which a customer need or desire is being met?
- *Uniqueness.* Does it measure some effectiveness characteristic that no other measure encompasses?
- *Completeness.* Does the list of measures cover all or at least most objectives?
- *Comprehensibility.* Is the measure understandable?
- *Cost.* Are cost and staffing requirements for data collection reasonable?
- *Timeliness.* Can the data be obtained quickly enough so that managers and staff can act on it before the information becomes obsolete?
- *Accuracy and Reliability.* Can sufficiently accurate and reliable information be obtained (Hatry, Blair, Fisk, Greiner, Hall & Schaenman, 1992)?

Most importantly, performance measurement data should be perceived by program managers and other decision makers as tied meaningfully to the budget process. As Ammon (1999) cautions "unless those measures are something more than decorations for the budget document, as superficial reporting practices have been called derisively – any enthusiasm for measurement will quickly lose its luster, and probably deserve to (pp. 106–107). Yet to integrate strategic planning and performance measures into the budget process as prescribed under performance budget reform is not a simple process.

Adoption In the States

Because of the time pressures in the budget process, many states' performance budgeting initiatives are part of a statewide strategic planning process (NCSL, 1994, p. 3). Goals achieved through legislative consensus are often so global (i.e. improve educational quality) or so diffused (i.e. the aggregate of stated or implied goals for each component of a program) that they provide little direction in determining explicit measures needed to establish a performance budgeting system (GAO, 1997). Statewide strategic plans establish priorities and determine what should be the outcomes of programs over the longer term. They also provide a method for linking the mission, vision and goals of agency programs to annual spending decisions (Berry & Weschler, 1995; CFO Council, 1997; NASBO, 1996). These statewide plans have been established in a variety of ways: by using a task force of community leaders and the public, committees comprised of legislators and administrators, as well as strategic planning efforts of program managers.

In state government, some of the foremost examples of strategic plans are Minnesota Milestones, Texas Tomorrow, and Oregon Benchmarks. Although the specifics of these performance-based models vary across jurisdictions, they commonly include several identifiable steps: (1) strategic planning to determine goals, (2) the definition of programs and activities in terms of how they contribute to these broad policy goals, (3) the establishment of performance measures as indicators of progress, and (4) the monitoring and reporting of these measures as part of the budget cycle (Broom, 1996; Broom & McGuire, 1995; CFO Council, 1997; Wholey & Hatry, 1992).

While there is general agreement, though not consensus, that public budgeting would be improved by linking funding decisions to performance measures, there is considerable debate about how this can be done. The Office of the Legislative Auditor for the State of Minnesota (1994) lists some of the problems:

(1) It is unclear whether the appropriate budgetary response to a poorly performing program is to reduce its funding or increase it,
(2) program performance may depend on factors that are outside of an agency's control or that are not easily measured,
(3) tying funding to performance could create incentives for misreporting, and
(4) budgeting is a political process of making choices and tradeoffs, not merely a mechanical process for allocating funds based on data or formulas (p. xiv).

Programs further face administrative tasks of varying scope and difficulty that change over time. A larger program, one with more complex administrative apparatus or one in which administration must be conducted under constraints from outside actors, such as the courts, may require more resources simply to achieve as much as can be achieved with fewer resources in another (Elling, 1992, Chap. 6). In addition, the nature of many governmental activities is such that the accomplishments in relation to costs cannot be precisely measured even after the fact (Lewis, 1952). There is also difficulty in determining how a program's objectives can be translated into specific measures for a short term budget cycle since an annual or biannual budget cycle is often too short a time frame to observe results (Wholey & Hatry, 1992).

Because there are no perfect solutions to these and other implementation issues, governments have adopted various forms of performance-based budgeting operating at different stages of development. Some states are using performance measures in budget documents for information purposes, others such as Texas formally link program outcomes to funding recommendations or, as is the case in Arizona, to program retention, elimination or modification.

States also vary in how they perceive performance based changes to their budget process. For example, Louisiana (Louisiana Office of Planning & Budget, 1996) identifies their process of "budgeting for results" as "program budgeting" (p. OP&B-1) supported by "performance accountability" (p. A-1) whereas Utah (King, 1996) classifies their use of performance measures in budgeting as a "strategic planning process that is performance-based" (p. 6). Other states, (e.g. Missouri and Pennsylvania) consider current initiatives to integrate measures of program results into budgeting as a continual development in long-term efforts to use performance measures in their budget process (Reading, 1996; Warfel, 1996).

The National Conference of State Legislatures (NCSL) (1994) defines performance-based budgeting in theory as "the allocation of resources to achieve specific objectives based on program goals and measured results" (NCSL, 1994, p. 2). Yet, the NCSL (1994, p. 9) acknowledges that in practice this is a budget process governments are moving toward and one that state governments may not yet have achieved. Others (e.g. Brown & Pyers, 1998; Franklin, 1999; Lee, 1997; Melkers & Willoughby, 1998) point out that the efforts to link performance and budgeting are a long-term process that has taken, and will continue to take, many years to be fully implemented.

For this reason, the definition of performance-based budgeting used in this study is broadened to include the systematic reporting of performance outputs and outcomes that reflect program goals and measures of their achievement as part of a state's annual or biennial budget process. Being "systematic" means that "key measures are selected in advance and reports on them are issued on a regular basis" (OECD, 1995, p. 54). State initiatives are also discussed in terms of "performance budget reform" which indicates the movement toward, not the achievement of, performance-based budgeting.

Based upon these definitions, forty of the fifty states have adopted performance budget reform. As shown in Table 1, states vary with respect to how reforms are implemented. The majority of states that have implemented reform report adopting a statewide approach applicable to all agencies and programs. Fewer states have used pilot projects or a phase-in of agencies or programs.

States also differ with respect to the characteristics of performance measures and how performance measurement data is integrated into the budget process. Table 2 illustrates that half of the states adopting performance budget reform publish performance measures in the budget document. More than half of the states also report performance measures at a program level. However, many states report measures on an agency and subprogram level as well. Performance measures are linked to agency and state strategic plans as often as they are linked to program missions and goals and while performance measures are most frequently compared to previous performance and internally established targets, many states do benchmark against similar organizations or the best organization. Measures typically cover three or four years and twenty three of the forty states that have adopted reform monitor these measures annually. However, half of the states report that they do not verify or audit performance measures.

Table 1. State Approaches Toward Implementing Performance Budget Reform.

State Approaches Toward Reform	Number of States	States
All agencies/programs	25	CN, DE, GA, HI, ID, IL, IN, LA, MS, MO, NE, NV, NH, NC, PA, OK, RI, TN, TX, UT, VT, VA, WA, WV, WY
Phase-in of agencies/ programs	10	AZ, FL, IO, KS, MI, MN, MT, NM ND, OH,
Pilot projects	5	AK[1], CA, KY, ME[2] NJ
No budget reform initiative	10[3]	CO, OR, SC, SD[4] AL, AR, MD, MA, NY, [5]WI

[1] AK: All agencies have departmental measures in place as of FY 97. Agency-level and program-level measures will be developed over the next one to two years.

[2] ME: Initiative requires all agencies to select a pilot program for FY 98/99 biennial budget with full implementation for 2000–01 biennium.

[3] State programs may report performance measures but on an ad hoc basis. States may centrally direct the reporting of performance measurement data but there is no ongoing initiative to incorporate this information into the budget process.

[4] SD: Performance budgeting statute passed during previous governor's administration but is not presently being implemented.

[5] NY: Formally incorporated a performance measurement system in its budget process in 1981. However, the law establishing "Key Item Reporting System" (KIRS) was repealed in 1992 as it was determined KIRS did not have significant impact on budgetary decisions.

Decentralizing Control and Cutting Red Tape

Whereas traditional budgeting emphasized input control and top down rules, under performance budgeting, control is exercised by establishing objectives, translating them into quantitative indicators and holding budget units accountable for results (Wholey & Hatry, 1992). There are more stringent requirements for budget units to achieve specified goals but greater discretion as to the means used to obtain them (Cothran, 1993; GAO, 1997; National Performance Review, 1993b, 1997; OECD, 1994, 1995, 1997; Roberts, 1997).

Table 2. Characteristics of Performance Measurement Data in States' Budgets.

Characteristics of Performance Measurement Data	States With Budget Reform Initiative	States Without Budget Reform Initiative
Where published		
Budget document	20	4
Budget supplement	3	0
Separate Performance Report	6	2
Budget document & Separate report	6	0
Not published	5	0
Not apply	0	4
Level Reported		
Agency	4	1
Program	14	0
Subprogram	4	0
Agency & subprogram	8	3
Program & subprogram	5	1
Agency, program & subprogram	5	1
Not apply	0	4
Linked to strategic plans		
Statewide missions/goals	2	0
Agency mission/goals	8	1
Program mission/goals	9	0
Agency & program mission/goals	12	2
State & agency or program mission/goals	3	0
State, agency & program mission/goals	6	1
Not apply	0	6

Table 2. Continued.

Characteristics of Performance Measurement Data	States With Budget Reform Initiative	States Without Budget Reform Initiative
Standards against which measures are compared		
Previous performance	8	3
Preset targets	1	0
Previous performance & targets	14	1
Previous performance, targets and/or similar organizations	3	0
Previous performance, targets and/or best organizations	2	0
Previous performance, targets, similar & best organizations	11	0
Other	1	
Not apply	0	6
Number of years measures cover		
1	1	2
2	2	0
3	11	1
4	10	2
5 or 6	2	0
7, 8, or 10	6	0
Varies	8	1
Not apply	0	4
Who monitors		
Agency	5	2
Exec. budget office	4	0
State Auditor	1	0
Agency & Exec. budget office	6	0
Agency, Exec. budget office, & Leg. budget office	14	3
Agency, Exec. budget office, & state auditor	2	0
Agency, Exec. budget office, Leg. budget office & auditor	7	1
Other	1	0
Not apply	0	4
Frequency monitored		
Biennially	7	0
Annually	23	5
Quarterly	3	0
Annually & quarterly	2	1
Other	5	0
Not apply	0	4
Who verifies		
Exec. budget office	9	0
Leg. budget office	4	0
State Auditor	5	0
Exec. budget office, & Leg. budget office	2	0
Not apply	20	10

The reasons for these changes are both practical and conceptual. Today, there exists a vast network of regulations and procedures to control the behavior of government officials which can detect error and prevent the abuse of discretion. However, rules and regulations can also result in red tape, lack of flexibility and inefficiencies which frustrate administrators and impede their ability to respond to public problems. Bureaucratic patterns of work are considered to be "hidebound, rule oriented, and generally uneconomic" (Premchand, 1998, p. 82). While no government agency wants to be rule-bound and sluggish, it occurs through the steady buildup of layers over time (National Commission on State and Local Public Service, 1993, p. 361).

The National Academy of Public Administration (NAPA) (1983) made a similar point a decade earlier in its call for deregulating federal management. According to the NAPA panel:

> Over many years, government has become entwined in elaborate management control systems and the accretion of progressively more detailed administrative procedures, often heavily centralized. This development has not produced superior management. Instead, it has produced managerial overburden. . . . Procedures overwhelm substance. Organizations become discredited, along with their employees. . . . The attitude of those who design and administer the rules . . . must be reoriented from a 'control mentality' to one of 'how can I get the mission of this agency accomplished (pp. vii, viii).

In contrast to the early principles on which the executive budget was founded, that is, countering political influence and rationalizing administration by means of hierarchy and standardization of procedures, today's advocates of reform are focused on "debureaucratization". The rigidity of bureaucracy is considered particularly damaging today, a time when complexity and change in modern society is escalating and when government needs to display increasing agility (DiIulio, Garvey & Kettl, 1993, OECD, 1994, 1995, 1997; Premchand, 1998).

Much of what government now does it does through institutions and individuals beyond its immediate control. This is evident in the delegation of responsibility to other levels of government and to non-government organizations by means of grants, subsidies, and loans. Moreover the growing interest in privatization has accelerated the trend to delegate or contract out activities to the private sector (Berry, Brower & Flowers, 2000; Bundt & Lutz, 1999). Such diffused authority makes accountability much more complex and reliance on top-down control systems less feasible.

Furthermore, just as dispersed and shared responsibility in government is a reality, so too are fiscal constraints. Governments at all levels are under pressure to do more with less and better satisfy the citizen/taxpayer while doing it (Hale & Hyde, 1994; Ingraham & Romzek, 1994; National Commission on the State and Local Public Service 1993; National Performance Review, 1993a,

Osborne & Gaebler, 1992; Radin, 2000). Whereas earlier budget reforms emphasized improved performance through the systematic assessment of alternative programs (e.g. PPBS) or different funding levels for the same program (e.g. ZZB), a principal aim of performance budgeting is to generate budget savings by reducing red tape and promoting "entrepreneurial behavior by public administrators" (Cothran, 1993, p. 445). As a commission member for the study of reform in Wisconsin put it: "There are billions to be saved when we remove the process barriers and let people serve the mission by being held accountable to results and not process" (Wisconsin Commission For the Study of Administrative Value & Efficiency, 1995, p. 75).

This perspective is also reflected in the National Performance Review Report (1993a) on reinventing the federal government:

> Today, the central issue we face is not *what* government does, but *how* it works. We have spent too much money for programs that don't work. It's time to make our government work for the people, learn to do more with less, and treat taxpayers like customers. . . . The problem is not lazy or incompetent people; it is red tape and regulation so suffocating that they stifle every ounce of creativity. . . . Effective, entrepreneurial governments cast aside red tape, shifting from systems in which people are accountable for following rules to systems in which they are accountable for achieving results (pp. 2, 6).

Similar themes of reducing red tape and decentralizing control were expressed in forums across seven states sponsored by the National Commission on the State and Local Public Service (1995). Max Sherman, Commission member and former dean of the Lyndon B. Johnson School of Public Affairs summarizes their findings as follows:

> Somewhere we've got to recapture the ability to do things right the first time. We the voters and citizens are saying 'enough'. In making it difficult to steal the public's money, we have made it impossible to manage the public's money. In attempting to control everything, we became so obsessed with dictating how things should be done – regulating the process, controlling the inputs – that we have ignored the outcomes and results (p. 3).

Tight control over resource inputs is a major strength of traditional, line-item budgeting. Object classes are intended to report obligations "by the initial purpose for which they are incurred rather than for the end product or service provided" (U.S. Office of Management and Budget, 1993, p. 125). The principal objective in adopting this budget format was to prevent "public funds from being stolen, used for unauthorized purposes, or spent at uncontrolled rates" (Betram, 1978, p. 147). But, now it is considered symptomatic of the "management control systems, technologies, and processes of a bygone era" (Leonard, Cook & McNeil, 1995, p. 5).

In today's world of globalization and rapid environmental change, line-item budgeting is thought to be one of the foremost impediments toward achieving performance improvement (Barzelay, 1992; Durant, 2000; Osborne & Gaebler, 1992; Rosen, 1993). The requirement that unspent funds be returned to the general fund for reallocation is cited as providing little incentive for either economy or innovation (DiIulio, Garvey & Kettl, 1994; Mosso, 1999; Rosen, 1993; Thompson, 1993). Furthermore, compliance with top-down rules and adherence to objects of expenditure are criticized for inhibiting responsiveness to customers and limiting the ability to shift resources to meet changing problems and opportunities (NCSL, 1994, p.2).

According to Landau and Stout (1979), a hierarchical approach to control undermines the ability to intelligently respond to change because it impedes organizational learning. Control systems that "build on the foundations of compliance provide protection against infraction of rules but not against error" (p. 153). Problems are not eliminated or ameliorated by the imposition of directives. On the contrary, they prevent the search for adequate solutions by suppressing risk-taking and limiting the ability to detect and correct error. The price paid for this form of control is high. "Errors", they point out, "are information. Compliance is not. . . . Compliance, a synonym for obedience, may measure acquiescence or submission but it provides no information about outcomes and consequences" (p. 153).

A compliance approach to accountability does not enable individuals and their organizations to learn from experience, that is, to improve their understanding, on the basis of observed results, about what works, what doesn't, and why (Kettl, 1994, p. 21; Landau & Stout, 1979, p. 154). In the absence of such learning, public organizations and individuals simply repeat old practices rather than adapt to the varying uncertainties and problems they confront.

DiIulio, Garvey and Kettl (1993) present a stronger attack against the rules and regulations of top-down controls arguing that "we have built a system that maximizes control but delivers little accountability" (p. 27). Instead, bureaucracy has become more inner directed and rule-driven making it appear to be self-serving, not a servant of the public. What is required, they argue is an alternative appproach that encourages government officials to assume personal responsibility for government performance (pp. 24–28).

While government's rules and regulations serve important purposes, growth in the of number of rules and inflexibility in regulations can develop into increasingly formal-rational models of administration that turn dysfunctional and counterproductive (G. E. Caiden, 1991, p. 124, Dubnick, 1994, p. 259, Durant, 2000, p. 79; National Performance Review, 1993c, pp. 10–11; Premchand, 1998, p. 82; Wilson, 1989, p. 369). These "bureaupathologies" are not the personal failings of administrators but shortcomings of the organization.

Bureaucratic requirements, designed to preclude unfairness or error, develop into convoluted systems that cripple the exercise of human judgment and bring about bureaucratic complacency and inertia (G. E. Caiden, 1991, p. 124; Horner, 1994, p. 91). Regulations can reinforce the incentive for public managers to worry more about constraints than tasks (Thompson, 1994, p. 313; Kettl, 1994, p. 75). Procedures that have been designed to check abuses by closely monitoring workers can breed discouragement and indifference (DiIulio, Garvey & Kettl, 1993, p. 65; Rosen, 1989, p. 194).

Also, as government becomes increasingly complex and obstacles multiply, "just following regulations" can become the protection of the risk-averse who retreat behind bureaucratic procedures instead of addressing the issues (Garvey & DiIulio, 1994, p. 23). Moreover, as Kaufman (1977) notes, "when there are multitudinous categories and definitions, shrewd operators can find somewhere in the stack justification for almost anything they want to do" (p. 87). A consequence, is that today's reform confronts the dual problems of "over-control and underaccountability" (Leonard, Cook & McNeil, 1995, p. 5).

III. ACCOUNTABILITY, DISCRETION, AND REFORM: A FOCUS ON RESULTS

Performance budgeting proposes to rectify both overcontrol and under-accountability by changing the nature of accountability from compliance with rules toward accountability for results. The reform prescribes greater administrative discretion and support for entrepreneurial behavior in order to enable administrators to do their best with the resources at hand. However, the tension between discretion and accountability has long been discussed in public administration literature. Moreover, today's broadened conception of accountability and new directions in budget theory illustrate a remarkable convergence of outlook. Both reflect the ambiguity of governance in a system of shared powers and provide a theoretical basis for questioning the expectations of performance budget reform.

This chapter begins by reviewing the relationship of accountability and discretion as discussed in the literature. The theoretical basis for questioning the expectations of today's reform are then examined: first, in terms of traditional criticisms of reform initiatives or the politics of budgeting and second, in terms of new directions in budget theory and alternative conceptions of accountability which describe constraints to discretion that are largely outside the scope of budget reform. Finally, studies of reform are reviewed and hypotheses proposed which will be the basis of inquiry into practitioners' perceptions of accountability and discretion in the implementation of this reform.

ACCOUNTABILITY AND ADMINISTRATIVE DISCRETION

Accountability seems by definition to be a relationship of dependence. Its very meaning is a showing, or an obligation to show, that an agent has done what he or she had been told to do. The meaning of discretion is that the officer or agent has not been told what to do with the authority granted and consequently is free to choose. Therefore, the more there is of one, the less there is of the other (Mansfield, 1982, p. 61).

As Mosher (1982) points out "accountability is not commonly associated with invention . . . but rather with executing assignments which are more or less specifically defined, honestly, efficiently, effectively, and at minimal cost" (p. 72). Thus at the very outset, there is a conflict between the values associated with accountability and the values of discretion, innovation, and entrepreneurship advanced by reform.

Defined in traditional terms, accountability does breed such conflicts. Early Taylorite principles, reflected a desire to control if not eliminate the discretionary authority of administrators. Wilson, Taylor, Weber and Gulick maintained that institutional arrangement mattered and that a bureau's hierarchical design, and a bureaucrat's performance and accountability were interrelated. By establishing clear lines of authority, matching responsibility to authority, and providing for functional specialization, efficiency (the primary objective) would be realized and control (a basic tenet of accountability) enhanced.

Dwivedi and Jabbra (1988) contend that the traditional concept of accountability considers public officials and their organizations accountable "only to the extent that they are legally required to answer for their actions" (p. 5). Paul Light (1993) labels this "compliance accountability" which he describes as an "effort to assure conformity with carefully drawn rules and regulations" (p. 3). In this sense, to be accountable is to report, explain, give reason, and to submit to an outside or external judgment. The role of oversight is primarily detection of error and the enforcement of negative sanctions (pp. 13–15).

In contrast, Light describes "performance accountability" as focusing on goal setting. The role of oversight is defined in terms of evaluation and benchmarking and the emphasis is on positive incentives (p. 14). Campbell (1994) also emphasizes goals, defining "performance accountability" as "judging the success of a policy or program by measuring its outcomes or results against agreed-upon standards" (p. 24).

These added dimensions of accountability acknowledge that, when public officials and their organizations are delegated responsibility, they require definition of objectives, flexibility and sufficient resources to achieve what is asked. That is, accountability plays a greater role than is indicated by the idea of direct and formalistic responses to top down control. It can also be understood as a shared responsibility.

OECD (1994) reports that its member countries have found the successful management of public organizations implies such an alternative approach to control. Instead of "traditional steering", control becomes an instrument for promoting "full accountability" or "demonstrated results whose origin can be explained" (p. 58).

Under this system, accountability is based on knowing results and being able to attribute them to a person (individual responsible), organization (collective responsible) or cause (making it possible to modify activities). The focus is on the quantitative and qualitative measurement of difference between initial objectives and observed results. By monitoring this variance, central units can ensure accountability and reward or penalize the unit concerned. The concept is one of confirming that the organization is "under control", or operating the way it should (p. 79).

A positive outcome of this approach, is that accountability loses its inquisitorial character and that agency management tools (e.g. performance measures) and control become more complementary. Individuals and their organizations are granted more freedom in their operations in return for accepting responsibility to attain specific objectives. Granting managers and others more discretion and flexibility provides them opportunities to adapt and creatively respond to changing needs.

These changing definitions are consistent with Barzelay's (1992) post-bureaucratic perspective:

> According to the bureaucratic paradigm, a key role of administrators was to use their authority to enforce responsibility upon their subordinates . . . And the notion of enforcing responsibility gave accountability a retrospective and defect-finding cast.
>
> From a post-bureaucratic perspective, the most effective way to hold employees accountable is to make them feel accountable. . . . the post-bureaucratic paradigm values efforts by public managers and their overseers to bring about states of affairs in which public servants feel accountable for achieving desired results (pp. 127–128).

Under this postbureaucratic approach, as attention moves away from ensuring compliance, central staff is free to develop greater steering capability over the organization's direction. Operating units are granted increased autonomy and the tensions between accountability, discretion, and innovation become more soluble (Barzelay, 1992, p. 119; Dubnick, 1994, p. 262; Roberts, 1997, p. 468).

Performance budgeting presumes such a reconciliation of tensions by proposing greater discretion while claiming that accountability is strengthened, albeit refocused. Central budget staff and policy makers maintain "control over the *total* amount" and "priorities" of spending, while requiring greater monitoring and evidence of program achievement (Cothran, 1993, p. 450). In exchange, program administrators are given considerably more discretion over how they spend their appropriated funds.

Some types of discretion envisioned under performance budgeting include administrator's ability to carry over funds from one year to the next, greater flexibility in determining the timing or allotment of funds, the capacity to generate and retain income and the possibility of retaining within the unit some or all of any savings made (Cothran, 1993, p. 450; Forsythe, 1993, p. 419; OECD, 1994, p. 62; National Commission of State and Local Public Service, 1993, p. 396; National Performance Review, 1993b, pp. 32–35).

Another example of devolution of control is giving administrators greater freedom to determine how to distribute appropriated resources within their programs. This may be done through the use of lump sum appropriations or granting agencies authority to reprogram funds. In essence, controls and rules are shifted from ex ante, those executed before money is spent to ex post, implemented during or after spending (Jones & Thompson, 1993).[1]

The value of such a change has long been recognized. Normanton (1971) argued over twenty-five years ago that instead of issuing detailed orders to hold lower level officials accountable, administrators could be held accountable a posteriori, thus affording them the opportunity to prove themselves worthy of their responsibilities.

> This can be a more flexible and less burdensome way of coordinating administration with government than by the issue of multifarious commands from the centre. It allows greater independence at subordinate levels, and is by way of a guarantee rather than a system of remote control (p. 32).

Whether central budget staff and the legislature will embrace this approach to accountability and be willing to change their behavior is a key question in assessing the relationship between budget reform and discretion. It is also a question that is at the basis of traditional criticisms of reform.

TRADITIONAL CRITIQUE: THE POLITICS OF BUDGETING

Budget reform has long been criticized for its failure to consider the politics of budgeting (Joyce, 1993a; Pilegge, 1992; Radin, 2000; Roberts, 2000; Rubin, 1988, 1992; Schick, 1973, 1977, 1994a; Wildavsky, 1964, 1986, 1992a). Wildavsky, one of the foremost critics of rational-analytical approaches to reform, argued that far from being a neutral matter of "better budgeting", budget reform inevitably contained important implications for the political system, that is, "who shall receive budgetary benefits and how much"

(Wildavsky, 1992a, p. 595). This is not just a matter of maximizing results for budgetary expenditures. It is a matter of politics:

> Budget reforms are aimed at the wrong target. . . . If the present budgetary process rightly or wrongly is deemed unsatisfactory, then one must alter in some respects the political system of which the budget is but an expression. This task, however is inevitably so formidable that most reformers prefer to speak only of changing the budgetary process, as if by some subtle alchemy the intractable political element could also be transformed into a more malleable substance" (1992b, pp. 430–431).

While the political nature of budgeting is integral to contemporary approaches to budget theory (e.g. Bartle, 1999; N. Caiden, 1990; Rubin, 1988, 1992, 1993; Schick, 1994a; Whicker, 1992), the literature on performance budget reform, continues to downplay, if not ignore, political considerations. Harris (1995) charges that support for reporting output and outcome measures in state and local budgeting "is grounded in the same apolitical, mechanistic perspective as program planning budgeting (PPB), management by objectives (MBO), and zero based budgeting (ZBB)" (p. 25). The GAO (1997) maintains that these past initiatives demonstrate that budget reform "cannot be viewed in simple mechanistic terms since "the process of budgeting is inherently an exercise in political choice" (p. 4). Moreover, the GAO anticipates that "reaching a reasonable level of consensus on clear and precise strategic goals will almost certainly encounter political hurdles" (p. 11).

Many others share the view that reform cannot be divorced from politics and the political culture. Roberts (2000) argues that "discussion about specific targets for specific programs, specific agencies, and specific years is problematic" because "clarification requires politicians to choose from among competing constituencies" (pp. 306–307). Behn (1996) too notes that "clarifying objectives is managerially sound but politically irrational" as "it reintroduces political disagreements that have been carefully minimized by incorporating the vague (rather than precise) purposes into the authorizing legislation" (p. 18).

Joyce (1993b) also maintains that performance budget reform expects executive branch budget offices and the legislative body to change their behavior "from emphasizing front-end, micro-level inputs to emphasizing the big picture – the results obtained from public programs" (p. 13). While he agrees performance-based budgeting systems "may be desirable", Joyce (1993a) reiterates Wildavsky's criticism stating that "it is impossible to mandate that decision makers . . . actually use it" (p. 46).

Although there is much written about the logic of increased administrative discretion, there are few discussions that address how to demonstrate to a legislature or central budget staff the value of relinquishing control over public agencies (G. E. Caiden, 1994, p. 126; Cox, 1994; p. 109; Rosenbloom, 1993, p. 506). While cooperation among the legislature, central budget staff, and agencies is possible, the authoritative element in the relationship is clear. Agency administrators must comply with the guidelines of central budget staff, and central budget staff are subordinate to the legislature in the appropriation of public funds. The executive's central budget office can advance performance budgeting, but ultimately it is the legislature that declares a program's purpose, allocates resources and writes the law.

The changes proposed to advance reform, however, assume legislative authorization which may not be forthcoming (G. E. Caiden, 1994; Curro, 1995; Kettl, 1994; Khademian, 1995). According to Radin (2000) the passage of the Government Accounting and Results Act of 1993 was anticipated to depoliticize budgetary decision making and turn it into "an information-driven, technical, and rational process" (p. 112). However, he found instead:

> The experience of implementing the measure has not yielded anything approximating those expectations. In fact, the process has been far more contentious than anyone expected. And, in at least some situations, instead of leading to a more rational budget process, budgets for FY2000 have included more politically motivated set-asides than those of the previous year" (p. 112).

Indeed, micromanagement is often used purposively as a tool for legislative control of the executive branch (Rosenbloom, 1993, p. 505). Legislators may well resist relaxing controls over performance-based agencies.

For example in Florida, which considers itself "ahead of other states and the federal government in funding programs based on results" (Florida Office of Program Policy Analysis and Government Accountability, 1997, p.1), researchers found that departments have been "unsuccessful in getting policy makers to agree to initiatives for budget flexibility" (Berry, Brower & Flowers, 2000, p. 353). Instead, legislative budget decisions "continue to structure agencies' missions through line-item budgets" (Ibid., p. 356).

Elected officials may consider compliance more important than performance. They may not want to relinquish power to administrators if it is perceived to be at their own institution's expense or if they fear abuses that could result if rules were relaxed. Furthermore, even if politicians do agree to relinquish control, some argue public administrators should not be given more autonomy. From their perspective, the mission of a government agency is determined by representatives of the people, not agency management. The job of administration is to ensure that the government's power is used to execute the law, and control should not be transferred to administrators in a way that could undermine the democratic process (Arnold, 1995; Goodsell, 1993; Frederickson, 1992, 1996; Moe, 1994; Moe & Gilmour, 1995).

Wildavsky, who criticized apolitical approaches to reform because they didn't reflect the reality of budgeting, was also critical of reform initiatives on normative grounds. In his opinion, one should judge budget outcomes in terms of process, not the other way around. Reversing the relationship, as reformers insist, would require that one begin with "a theory that contains criteria for determining what ought to be in the budget, which would be nothing less than a theory stating what the government ought to do" (1992b, p. 129).

As this study focuses on practice, the normative discussion of whether discretion should be granted administrators is largely beyond the scope of the study. However, the question of to what extent public administrators should be responsive to external authority or exercise responsibility consistent with their own professionalism has a long and rich literature. Much of this discussion centers on the "best" strategy for achieving accountability with the exchange between Friedrich (1940) and Finer (1941) being the classic example.

While it is generally accepted in democracies that agency administrators must be accountable to constitutionally elected or delegated political overseers, the degree of answerability still remains controversial (Aberback & Rockman, 1988). In a review of what he terms "the perennial debate", Durant (1995) classifies the exercise of administrative discretion into three models: "whether professionals working within the bureaucracy should be *mavens* (relatively autonomous experts), *minions* (supplicants of elected officials), or *modified mandarins* (the synergist fusion of presidential leadership with an efficiency-inspired professional service)" (p. 167). He concludes that most of the discussions either take "an all-or-nothing approach (i.e. either political officials or experts should prevail across all circumstances)" or fail "to systematically and explicitly examine the issue" (p. 189). According to Durant, there needs to be a reframing of the debate in terms that further clarify and differentiate the issues.

CURRENT VIEWS: NEW THEORIES OF ACCOUNTABILITY AND BUDGETING

Contemporary theories of accountability and budgeting do offer a means for reframing the debate. Added to the limitations raised by the politics of budgeting, these approaches further differentiate checks on administrative discretion. Relative to budgeting, this literature indicates that reform is affected by multiple and often conflicting accountability claims and that the budget process is characterized by increasingly limited control over annual spending decisions.

Multiple Accountability Claims

Recent literature on accountability advances a broadened understanding as well as a refinement of the term. These conceptualizations move beyond the "all-or-nothing" approach of the normative debate to describe a condition wherein administrators control themselves through hierarchical and professional mechanisms at the same time they are subject to external restrictions (political forces and legal requirements).

Dwivedi and Jabbra (1988) present a model which distinguishes between general notions of performance consistent with societal norms and values and formal or operational compliance with specific legal mandates. Within this context, they list five types of accountability: organizational or administrative, legal, professional, political, and moral.

According to Dwivedi and Jabbra (1988) administrative accountability reflects a hierarchical relationship between the centers of responsibility and the units where orders are acted upon. Legal accountability relates actions in the public domain to the established legislative and judicial processes. Political accountability refers to the power of political authority to regulate, set priorities, and appropriate resources. Professional accountability reflects the standards of acceptable practice and ethics by which professional performance is evaluated. Finally, moral accountability relates to the principles acknowledged through constitutional and legal documents, and accepted by the public as established societal norms (pp. 5–8).

Romzek and Dubnick (1987, 1993, 1994) delineate similar professional and organizational standards of performance (bureaucratic, legal, professional, and political) but with a variation not found in the previous definition. They add that accountability "involves the means by which public agencies and their workers manage the diverse expectations generated within and outside the organization" (1987, p. 228). This definition introduces an element of control wherein administrators attempt to shape or participate in framing the standards by which they are judged.

Romzek and Dubnick propose that accountability mechanisms in the United States vary along two dimensions: source of control and degree of control. The source of control relates to the origin of expectations, whether internal or external, and the relationship of stakeholders to the agency or individual. The degree of this control can vary from high to low.

A high degree of control involves close specification of duties and scrutiny of actions across a wide range of issues. A low degree of control, in contrast, allows considerable discretion on the part of the agency or employee. The interplay of these two dimensions yields a typology of four categories of accountability mechanisms, each emphasizing different values and different bases for the accountability relationship.

Bureaucratic accountability mechanisms are characterized by a high degree of control by an internal source, typically a supervisor or rules of operation. The prevailing value is that of efficiency. Under this approach, expectations of public administrators are managed by focusing attention on the priorities of those at the top of the bureaucratic hierarchy. Accountability relationships are between a hierarchical positioned superior and a subordinate.

Legal accountability involves a high degree of scrutiny from an external source (e.g. a court or an outside auditor). Like the bureaucratic form, it involves the frequent application of control to a wide range of activities. However, it is based on a contractual relationship between a controlling party outside the agency, and members of the organization. The relationship implies a formal or fiduciary (principal/agent) agreement between the subordinate and the overseer holding the rule of law as the central value.

Professional accountability is characterized by a low degree of scrutiny and an internal source of control. It occurs with greater frequency as an organization deals with technically difficult and complex problems. Under these circumstances, public officials place control over activities in the hands of those with the expertise or special skills to get the job done. The key relationship is similar to one between a lay person and an expert with the dominant value being deference to expertise.

Political accountability also involves a low degree of scrutiny from an external source (e.g. a citizens' group or elected officials). The central relationship under these systems resembles that between a representative and his constituents with the prevailing value being responsiveness. Under both political and professional accountability systems. the agency or individual has greater discretion than under either bureaucratic or legal accountability mechanisms to decide how best to respond to expectations. In theory, Romzek and Dubnick claim each of these alternative accountability systems is equally legitimate, and all may be present in an organization even if some are not used.

O'Loughlin (1990) includes the central logic of Romzek and Dubnick's model but rejects the "management of expectations" concept as a core phenomenon in accountability relationships:

> When we speak about bureaucratic accountability, the bottom line is that we are concerned about whether or not our government agencies are under some control and oversight by us or our representative institutions. . . . We are not primarily concerned with whether or not administrators can effectively "manage expectations". To the contrary this may be what we fear (p. 281).

Instead, O'Loughlin develops more fully the traditional concept of accountability as "answerability" while incorporating political, legal, and to some extent professional systems of accountability. He proposes that accountability relationships between bureaucracies and other representative governmental and non-governmental organizations involve: (1) effective communication systems through which bureaucratic explanations of actions and decisions to outside actors occur; (2) outside actor influence over bureaucratic decision making; and (3) discretionary and non-discretionary spheres of decision making.

Legal authority is viewed by O'Loughlin as "one source of power which helps to define the discretionary and non-discretionary spheres of decision making" (p. 282). For example, statutory authority gives elected officials a potential source of power over agency decision making. This focus is similar to Romzek and Dubnick's (1987) explanation of legal accountability as an "outside party . . . in a position to impose legal sanctions or assert formal contractual obligations" (p. 229).

His model's delineation of discretionary and non-discretionary spheres of decision making also incorporates the central logic of Romzek and Dubnick's "professional" accountability system insofar as "in any accountability relationship, worthy of its name, . . . discretionary spheres of decision-making power must be present if efficiency and technical expertise are to be maximized" (p. 282). O'Loughlin thus views bureaucracies "expert abilities to deal with public problems" as the basis of administrative discretion not as an alternative accountability relationship (p. 282). In his framework, the central questions are: "Over what decisions and actions do outside actors exercise influence? To what extent?" (p. 281).

This "responsiveness" emphasis fits closely with Romzek and Dubnick's political accountability category but O'Loughlin incorporates it into the answerability tradition, "keeping responsiveness to outside actors as the central spirit of accountability" (p. 281).

The conceptions of accountability and administrative discretion defined by O'Loughlin are those used in this study. Professional accountability is considered implicit in the meaning of administrative discretion. That is, administrative discretion is conceived as administrators' ability to exercise their own judgement and professional expertise in decision making. Accountability is also considered to be answerability to outside claims or demands, not management of expectations. However, to a lesser degree, Romzek and Dubnick's concept that administrators must deal with multiple accountability demands is accepted, by proposing that administrators "balance" rather than "manage" these demands.

Acknowledging that administrators balance multiple accountability claims makes explicit the plurality of interests involved in any change. This is an important, though overlooked, consideration in normative theories of budget reform. Public administrators are answerable to elected officials and political appointees, legislative bodies, and the courts. Associated with these actors are different mechanisms for ensuring accountability and different views as to what accountability means.

Administrators confront political values of representativeness and responsiveness, a legal focus on equity, individual rights and due process along with managerial attention to efficiency and effectiveness (Rosenbloom, 1983, 1993). As Barth (1993) observed in a study of federal administrators, although they did not explicitly think of their jobs in constitutional terms, "public administrators are engaged in a struggle to maintain an order consistent with the delicate balance that is a fundamental aspect of our constitutional form of government" (p. 177).

Kaufman (1996) makes a similar observation in reflecting on his writings about the sources of, and remedies for red tape stating that he essentially was "describing the way the government works" (p. 136). He argues "that responsibility for the massive outpouring of government requirements and restraints decried as red tape is widely shared", not because "we manufacture red tape deliberately", but because "every restraint and requirement originates in somebody's demand for it" (1977, p. 29).

> Unquestionably, they [public administrators] are tightly constrained. Their discretion is legally limited by statutes, regulations of sister agencies, judicial decisions, executive orders, and departmental directives. It is also politically limited by the need to accommodate powerful political figures and influential interest groups . . . (pp. 25–26).

Based upon a study of entrepreneurship among public managers, Moon (1999) agrees finding that "organizations with heavy legal constraints tend to have more red tape in order to protect themselves from potential political and legal liabilities" (p. 40). Peters and Savoie (1996) outline what some of these liabilities are:

> First, there are a number of personnel and structural requirements that cannot be easily eliminated. . . . For example, even if the personnel system is changed to make it more like that of the private sector, there are still legal requirements for merit selection and numerous protections against arbitrary dismissal. There are also programmatic requirements by which government agencies must abide when they make and implement their policies. Government agencies may become more entrepreneurial and their employees more empowered, but the legal requirements remain and must be fulfilled or the agencies can expect to be challenged in the courts (p. 287).

Performance budgeting's contention that the reporting entity is accountable for being economical, efficient, and effective provides a limited basis for external accountability to legal or political overseers. Furthermore, as Harris (1995) points out, the assumed dominance of these managerial values ignores two critical questions:

> One question is, from whose perspective are economy, efficiency, and effectiveness to be judged? ... Responding to this question introduces a missing value, equity, which is a fundamental public-sector value... The other critical question is, how does one move from information about entity unit performance to judgments about the relative values of expenditures for different purposes? This is a fundamental question with respect to budgeting theory ... (Harris, 1995, pp. 22–23).

New Directions in Budget Theory

There is now no widely accepted, central budget theory to answer the fundamental question: "On what basis shall it be decided to allocate x dollars to activity A instead of activity B" (Key, 1940, p. 1137). However, the current literature on budget theory offers insight into a budget process where control over spending decisions is increasingly limited. Prior years' spending commitments often eclipse annual appropriation decisions and program funding is determined by various means (e.g. federal mandates, formulas, or users' fees), all which serve to limit discretion.

Added to the traditional understanding of the politics of budgeting, today's budget theorists also emphasize: fiscal constraints (Levine & Rubin, 1980; Rubin, 1988, 1992, 1993, 1995); top-down, macro-budgeting generated by revenue limitations, intergovernmental mandates, and the courts (Axelrod, 1989; Bunch & Straussman, 1993; Hackbart & Carson, 1993; LeLoup, 1988); as well as the impact of multiyear, legal entitlements to funding (Straussman, 1986, 1988).

In recent years, multiyear spending decisions built into the structure of many programs, particularly entitlements, have limited discretionary spending.[2] These entitlements have also expanded the participants in the budget process to recipients who have a direct stake in the outcomes. As a consequence, the group of actors who play a role in budgeting has been broadened to include interest groups and the courts.

Court decisions and intergovernmental mandates now are recognized as impacting funding levels for programs. Earmarked revenues also influence how much is spent. A conception of budgeting based upon a stable, predictable process recurring annually no longer applies. Instead, the budget process is perceived as complex, fragmented, multisourced, and multiyear. Economic constraints and the heightened sensitivity of the budget to changes in growth rates, inflation, and unemployment, furthermore, hold spending hostage to forces it cannot always control or accurately predict.

Straussman (1986, 1988) examines the need to differentiate, what he terms "rights-based" appropriations from regular spending. These expenditures are made because there is a societal belief that people are entitled to a level of service by some moral or legal right. He argues that rights-based budgeting and the assumption about discretion and choice in budgetary processes may distort what, in fact, is a more restrictive reality. For example, entitlements have permanent appropriations. Congress cannot exert budget control without changing the language of authorization. Moreover, the courts have been sympathetic to the idea that beneficiaries should receive procedural due process protection before an entitlement may be withheld.

State and local governments, like the federal government, have also found that an increasingly larger portion of their budgets have been "earmarked" for rights-based programs due to actions taken by the courts. While rights-based claims are often thought of in terms of federal entitlement programs, other programs produce claims on the public purse that are less than absolute (e.g. education). For this reason, the conception of budgeting as an allocation process that determines preferences, or that emphasizes its decision-making features is extended to recognize different ways of looking at categories of expenditures.

Another movement in budget theory has been the shift in emphasis from micro to macro-budgeting. Macro-budgeting sets priorities centrally and works within constraints set by an external environment. The budget process is top-down in an effort to gain greater control over aggregate levels of taxing and spending (Lee, 1991, 1992, 1997; LeLoup, 1988; Sorensen, 1994).

At the state level, Bunch and Straussman (1993) find there has also been a shift toward macro-budgeting and in general, less budgetary discretion in spending. Legal limits, such as those on taxes, expenditures and debt, serve as top-down methods to control growth in spending. Base level adjustments, including inflation factors, collective bargaining increases, and civil service salary adjustments, require further top-down fiscal control to enforce balanced budget rules.

In addition, continued concern exists for achieving an acceptable balance for providing public services and paying for them within an intergovernmental framework. State aid to local governments comprises a sizeable portion of state spending. At the same time, budget decisions are impacted by federal incentives, disincentives, cross-cutting dictates and guidelines, and a host of other actions collectively referred to as "federal mandates" (Hackbart and Carson, 1993, p. 126). For example researchers in Florida found:

> As the [budget reform] implementation process unfolded, agency leaders soon realized that budget structures posed a major barrier to intraorganizational flexibility. As one explained,

> 'The budget systems encourages discrete program separation because of the restrictions, especially with federal dollars, on what you can spend money for. And contracting rules probably have as much to do with it as budgeting rules. Most of our work is done by private providers, and contracting rules from the state and federal governments regulate how those contracts are done' (Berry, Brower & Flowers, 2000, p. 348).

A somewhat different perspective on fiscal constraints is provided by studies on retrenchment. This literature differentiates budget processes according to revenue availability (or lack thereof) and describes how budget systems and actors are influenced (e.g. Behn, 1985; Bozeman & Straussman, 1982; Levine & Rubin, 1980; Straussman, 1979; Wilson & Sylvia, 1993).

Fiscal constraints brought on by the combination of economic conditions, taxpayer resistance and an ever increasing demand for services has focused attention on alternative ways to shift the burden of funding and/or provision of public services. Discussions have focused on the use of enterprise funds, user fees, privatization and an array of other mechanisms to increase alternative funding sources or to shrink the number of services government provides (Smith, 1999; Premchand, 1998).

Although these new directions in budget theory have not coalesced into a single school of thought, they have moved toward a common understanding of the major elements in reconceptualizing the budget process: annual and multiyear decisions with varying degrees of controllability, differentiated types of expenditures having various legal spending claims, a broadened conception of who plays a role in budgeting as well as the degree to which it is centralized, and the significance of fiscal constraints on budgetary decision making (Axelrod, 1989; Caiden, 1990; LeLoup, 1988; Rubin, 1988, 1992; Straussman, 1988).

The Linkage of Current Theories

A central theme in both literature streams of budget theory and accountability is that much of what occurs in public administration can be traced to the need of decision makers to be responsive to multiple accountability claims that involve diverse constraints.

In budgeting, judicial decisions as well as top-down expenditure ceilings and intergovernmental mandates add a legal dimension to the bureaucratic, political, and fiscal constraints that impact the budget process. Earmarked revenues require that funds be linked to specific programs. Multiyear spending decisions influence annual spending levels and heighten the sensitivity of budgets to changing economic conditions. Fiscal constraints, furthermore, restrict the choices available to public managers and reenforce an emphasis on spending targets and cutting costs. Yet, these factors remain outside the framework of reform.

Performance budgeting, however, does expect that bureaucratic and political accountability claims are to be changed. The reporting of performance measures is supposed to strengthen accountability for results, at the same time lessening the need for bureaucratic compliance with top-down rules. Reduction in rules, procedures, and reporting requirements is anticipated to provide greater discretion, streamlining the budget process and allowing administrators to utilize their expertise and to be more entrepreneurial, and thus, more efficient and effective.

Political accountability is also expected to be affected. Performance budget reform prescribes a devolution of control from policy makers and central budget staff to program administrators. Administrators are to be given more discretion to move money across line-items, granted increased flexibility in the timing of expenditures, and given the ability to carry over year-end surpluses to the new fiscal year. The assumption is also made that appropriations will be made with the focus on purchasing results rather than micromanaging costs and therefore legislatures will move away from line-item budgets and ex ante controls.

STUDIES OF BUDGET PROCESS REFORM

Although there has been a relatively major reform of the budget process proposed about once each decade since the 1950s, there has been little systematic study of the barriers to earlier initiatives. While there is no doubt that budgeting has changed during this period and that various reforms have contributed to this evolution, none of the reforms resulted in the wholesale changes in budgeting that each promised when enacted. Still, attention of budget reformers has generally been focused on the next innovation which is guaranteed to reinvent the process rather than assess prior efforts.

To a large extent, therefore, the literature on budget reform is comprised of either prescriptions for or descriptions of management innovations without examining why they have not been successfully implemented. There are recent studies where the implementation of budget reform has been examined systematically in select states. These typically have focused on whether changes in budget format have influenced the deliberations and decisions made by legislators and central budget staff or on what major factors are perceived to influence these actors.[3] Studies typically have not addressed how reforms affect budgetary decision making of administrators.[4]

Even so, this research does provide support for questioning the assumptions of performance budgeting as outline here. There is evidence that the legal basis of program funding as well as fiscal constraints are significant in budgetary decision making. The funding source (e.g. earmarked revenue, formula funding, and matching funds) was found to be such a recurring theme in budgetary deliberations of legislators, that it was added to the original conceptual framework examining budget reforms in Florida and North Carolina (e.g. Grizzle, 1986; Stanford, 1990, 1992).

After nearly a decade of work studying reform in Florida, Berry, Browner, and Flowers (2000) found that:

> Agency leaders soon discovered that PB [performance budgeting], tied as it was to existing budgeting channels, actually inhibited the flexibility they needed to define clients' needs holistically and in ways that addressed societal outcomes rather than agency outputs. They often found themselves defining client groups according to their designated funding streams rather than real societal needs (p. 348).

Willoughby (1992) also found that fiscal constraints in terms of the dollars available influenced the use of performance measures in the decision orientations of central budget staff in ten southern states. Duncombe and Kinney (1986) identified revenue availability as the most frequently mentioned factor perceived to affect state appropriations by executive and legislative budget staff in five western states (named by 77% of respondents). Interestingly, program performance, ranked tenth among thirteen major factors believed to affect legislative appropriations (named by 7% of the respondents).

In a nationwide survey of state executive and legislative budget officers, Abney and Lauth (1993) also discovered that fewer than half the budget officers surveyed (42%) reported that "an agency's reputation for efficiency in management of its activities" was a factor they considered when recommending agency budget requests and only 22% indicated an agency's effectiveness is relevant in gubernatorial decisions to increase the recommendations of the budget office (p. 47). While 58% of the executive branch respondents reported that "an agency's success in accomplishing its objectives" is a factor considered when reviewing agency requests, according to Abbey and Lauth, "it appears to operate more as a negative than a positive factor. That is, poor program management may get an agency into trouble more easily than effective management will help" (p. 47).

After surveying budget directors from each state executive budget office in 1997 Jordan and Hackbart (1999) concluded that "performance may impact the appearance and preparation of the budget document but the outcome in terms of funding is not significantly (if at all) affected" (p. 13). In percentage terms they found that "of the fourteen states that indicate that a performance-driven budget exists, ten of them indicate that as little as 3% or less of an agency's budget is performance driven. . . . This suggests that the actual impact of performance funding on an agency's total budget allocation is minuscule" (p. 13).

Willoughby and Melkers (2000) research is consistent with these findings. In a 1997 nationwide survey of state executive and legislative budgeters on the effects of performance-based budgeting, they found that budget reform was perceived as "somewhat effective" in improving government decision making, agency program results, and coordination between agencies and the legislature. However, they note:

> Generally, responses reflected a more cautious reaction to PBB [performance-based budgeting] than an enthusiastic one. Budgeters view PBB as less effective in reducing duplicative service and affecting cost savings and 'not effective at all' in appeasing the public and changing appropriations levels (p. 113).

A more positive perspective is offered by Franklin, Cawley and O'Sullivan-Katchel (1998) after reviewing the first two years of implementing Arizona's budget reform. This reform initiative is based upon a program authorization review (PAR) process which attempts to synthesize strategic planning, performance measurement, evaluation, and budgeting. The PAR process requires: (1) agency personnel's self-assessment of a program's performance based upon its strategic plan and performance measures; (2) budget analysts' (legislative and executive) review and recommendations in light of this self assessment and (3) legislative budgetary decisions to retain, eliminate or modify (REM) programs based upon the PAR findings.

Survey results indicated that "legislators, analysts, and agency representatives alike believe that the PAR process was beneficial" (p. 97). Regarding the benefits of the process, 75% of respondents felt that it evaluated the results of state programs while 59% thought it assessed needed changes in program operations or funding. However, a follow-up study conducted after five years of implementation found that there was limited use of performance information and that, as of 1998, it "did not have direct input into budget development" (Franklin, 1999 p. 203). While evaluation reports and program performance data were perceived as useful as reference documents, legislative committee staffers reported that this information had "little direct use in the appropriations process" (p. 203).

Bloom and McGuire (1995) reached a similar conclusion. After an in-depth study of five of the most progressive states in the implementation of performance budgeting (Texas, Oregon, Florida, Virginia, and Minnesota), they found that including performance measurement information in budget documents "adds value to deliberations", but "it does not appear to change the way budget decisions are made" (p. 14).

Case studies of select states by the Congressional Budget Office (CBO) (1993) and the General Accounting Office (GAO) (1993) also are not encouraging in terms of offering evidence that performance budget reform affects political decision making. Performance budget reform did not shift the appropriations process away from traditional, line-item budgeting despite long-standing efforts in some states. As Joyce (1993b) notes: "Neither the CBO visits to Florida and Oregon sites nor in depth studies by the GAO of five other states [Connecticut, Hawaii, Iowa, Louisiana, and North Carolina] identified any effect on the allocation of resources by the government in any state currently using performance measures" (p. 10). To date, neither Congress nor most state legislatures have exhibited a willingness to change the line-item format of their appropriation bills to match the program structure of reforms (CBO, 1993; GAO, 1993; Joyce, 1993a, 1993b; NASBO, 1990; NCSL, 1994).

This is not to suggest that Congress or state legislatures do not desire the information reported in performance budgets, only that this data is likely to add to, rather than replace, line-item reporting and oversight. The GAO (1994) notes that since the 1950 Budget Accounting and Procedures Act enacted the Hoover Commission's recommendations, Congress has required that both performance data and object class expenditures be included in the executive budget.

Relative to the Chief Financial Officers (CFO) Act of 1990 and the Government Performance and Results Act (GPRA) of 1993, the GAO (1994) finds that Congress has again "reaffirmed its commitment to performance-based oversight", however, it adds that "the implications of these initiatives on the need for and use of object-based information within the federal budget process remains an open question" (p. 10).

Commenting on the CFO Act, Jones (1993) is more pessimistic claiming: "Congress won't use the results produced by departments effectively except to increase oversight pressure and micromanagement to which executive department staff have become so accustomed" (p. 93). Carroll (1995) expresses similar opinions regarding the GPRA claiming that the "GPRA will proliferate red tape and increase Congress' oversight powers" (p. 306). Radin (2000) agrees citing Senator David Pryor's comments on the passage of GPRA: "My concern is that by mandating yet another very specific layer of internal management controls, performance measures and strategic plans, we are building in even more rigidity" (p. 117).

There is little indication at the state level reporting performance measurement data has significantly changed legislative oversight or increased agency flexibility. To the contrary, Berry, Browner and Flowers (2000) concluded that in Florida:

> Our evidence suggests that central budget control has been, by and large, sustained. Budget officials in one agency pointed out that they still prepare a line-item budget and carry it in boxes to legislative committee meetings, just as they did before. Those in another agency explained that they now prepare two budgets: a conventional line-item budget and a second one that ties program performance to their proposed budget allocations. Moreover, the reluctance of legislators to extend to the agencies the budget flexibility for incentives and disincentives outline in the law is instructive (p. 352–353).

In a review of all fifty states, Lee (1997) discovered that "despite all of the recent attention given to program information, budget offices reported a distinct decline in the use of such information in budget requests" (p. 135). Over the past twenty years there has been an increase in the inclusion of efficiency, and productivity (output) measures in budget documents (Lee, 1991, 1997). Yet, while 95% of states reported in 1990 that program effectiveness estimates were necessary when agencies asked for new programs or revisions in current ones, only 72% took that position in 1995. Similarly, reported use of productivity estimates (i.e. outputs) in budget requests declined from 86% of the states to 67% in 1995 (Lee, 1997; Lee & Burns, 2000). Even so this is still more than double the percentage in 1970 when only 29% of the states provided productivity measures and just 24% reported measures of effectiveness in their budget requests.[5]

Lee (1992) also found that with increased use of performance measurement information, state policy makers and central budget offices have increased their control over program priorities as well as their usage of guidance techniques for agencies' budget requests:

> Ranking of priorities, instructions to include necessary program improvements, instructions to maintain current services and instructions to maintain only minimum services are becoming standard. Following close behind these techniques are specific dollar-level ceilings. The days of agencies having the freedom to request budgets in whatever amounts they see fit are gone, and in their stead are various control mechanisms or types of ceilings that must be observed when requesting funds. (pp. 29–30).

Thompson (2000) calls this the "dual potentialities of performance measurement" (p. 267). He notes that on one hand performance measures can be used to enhance the capacity of managers to gain understanding of their operations. Alternatively, they can be used by top management to impose their own priorities and enhance their own power; that is, "the availability of measures has facilitated the ability of overseers to focus on and control specific program elements" (p. 275).

While more central direction over program "priorities" and "control over the total amount of spending" (Cothran, 1993, p. 449) is expected with the adoption of performance budgeting, compliance with more top-down rules and increases in reporting requirements are not consistent with an intent to reduce red tape. To the contrary, ever more rules and reporting requirements, especially if not used, are "pointless constraints" which are considered red tape of the worst kind (Kaufman, 1977, p. 8). Yet, this may be perceived to be the situation in performance budgeting.

While earlier surveys suggested that 60 to 80% of municipal jurisdictions in the United States use performance measures, Poister and Streib (1999) found that 40% or fewer "make any kind of meaningful use of performance measures in their management and decision processes" (p. 332). In a nationwide survey of state agencies examining reinvention reforms, Brudney, Hebert and Wright (1999) found that relatively few agencies (about 20 to 30%) of the 1200 agencies that responded report much progress in relaxing controls over administrative procedures (e.g. human resource rules, procurement rules, limitations on carrying over funds) even though these recommendations are central to reform efforts.

At the federal level, Jones and McCaffery (1993) argue that "there is little compelling evidence that Congress uses effectively the performance data it receives in great volume at present" (p. 73). Peters & Savoie (1996) conclude that, despite the changes promoted by the National Performance Review, the fundamental nature of central agencies in Washington, (i.e. the Office of Management & Budget, Office of Personnel Management and the General Services Administration) "has not been transformed and they are still very much in the business of imposing central controls" (p. 281).

SUMMARY

Although it has always been tempting for reformers to search for procedural changes and managerial solutions for perceived ills in budgeting, contemporary theories of accountability and budgeting provide a strong theoretical basis for questioning the expectations of performance budget reform. The politics of budgeting remains a formidable check on administrators using their professional expertise. Yet today, fiscal constraints and legal accountability claims are also recognized as limiting discretion in budgetary decision making but neither one of these restrictions is addressed within the scope of the theory. Furthermore, political accountability, if it isn't ignored, is assumed to be changed as reform dictates.

Studies of these initiatives also do not support the visions of change predicted by the normative theory. To the contrary, the findings suggest that there may not be a positive relationship between the implementation of reform and administrative discretion. Red tape could conceivably be increased by reform if, as these studies indicate, performance measurement information is added on to existing line-item reporting requirements and top-down guidance for budget preparation becomes more burdensome and restrictive. Likewise, if legislators and central budget staff use performance measurement as a negative tool to cut spending rather than as a justification for releasing administrators from ex ante controls, performance budgeting will promote more micro-management.

These studies also suggest that legal accountability claims and fiscal constraints need to be considered in assessing the changes that can be expected from performance budgeting. The amount of revenue available and its source have been found to be significant elements in budgeting. Moreover, these factors indicate that administrators may have little or no ability to influence a budget decision, much less be innovative in spending.

Based upon both the theoretical and empirical literature, it is expected that the performance budget reform may not be perceived to realize change in the manner prescriptive theory envisions. That is, administrators will not perceive a positive relationship between the implementation of performance budget reform and administrative discretion to the degree that: (1) the implementation of performance budget reform does not bring about the anticipated changes in bureaucratic and political accountability and, (2) legal accountability claims and fiscal constraints, which are beyond the scope of this reform, affect discretion in budget decision making.

NOTES

1. Jones and Thompson (1993) explain the distinction as follows: "Ex ante controls take the form of authoritative commands, executed and enforced by budget controllers, that tell government agencies or private sector service contractors what they may do, must do, or must not do. Examples include formal budget allotment orders or apportionments that regulate the rate of expenditure, fund and account controls that restrict transfer authority, and personal position controls. Ex post controls are implemented during or after spending – when costs have been incurred to make goods or services available. Since costs cannot be avoided after spending has occurred, ex post controls are intended to work by motivating service suppliers to make good decisions, that is, cost-effective or efficiency-producing choices" (p. 34).

2. Schick (1994b) maintains that at the federal level "controlling total expenditures is a much more difficult task today than it was a quarter century ago because much more of the budget is allocated to mandatory expenditures such as entitlements and interest charges. According to published OMB data, between 1965 and 1990 mandatory payments (many of which are open-ended) doubled as a percentage of total federal outlays, from 30 to 60%" (p. 7).

3. In addition to studies on the effect of budget process reform on deliberations and decisions of individual actors there are also studies addressing the implications of state budget reform on the balance of influence between the executive and legislative branch. For some examples see: Abney & Lauth, 1993, Saleh, 1991, and Thompson, 1987.

4. Although addressing budgeting in general, not its reform, Elling (1992) surveyed public managers in ten states and found that they perceived four of the ten most serious problems to management improvement were related to underfunding, that is, the tendency for legislatures to expand program responsibilities but not adjust appropriations (p. 184).

5. Lee's (1991) survey results also appear to run counter to a movement toward devolution of control. The proportion of states in which the central budget office exercised control over the transfer of funds from one object of expenditure to another rose from 59% in 1970 to 72% in 1990, increasing almost 10% from 1985 to 1990. Budget office control over program expenditures of appropriated funds also showed an increase from 19% in 1970 to 62% in 1990. Lee attributes these findings to the dramatic changes in the capabilities of centralized accounting systems to track transactions.

IV. STRUCTURING A STUDY OF THE STATES

The focus of this study is on examining the impact of performance budget reform at the state level. In particular, interest centers on the extent to which this reform is perceived to promote additional discretion for budget administrators affording them flexibility to better respond to change and achieve program goals.

Over the years, there have been repeated efforts to improve budgeting by implementing various reforms of the budgeting process (e.g. PPBS, MBO, and ZZB). Downs and Larkey (1986, p. 179) and others (e.g. Harris, 1995; Pilegge, 1992; Rubin, 1990; Schick, 1977; Wildavsky, 1986, 1992a) observe that the efforts were launched with great fanfare but fell far short of expectations. Initial examinations of performance budgeting reforms at the federal and state level do not indicate that today's reforms run counter to this pattern (Berry, Brower & Flowers, 2000; Broom & McGuire, 1995; Brudney, Hebert & Wright, 1999; Congressional Budget Office (CBO), 1993; General Accounting Office (GAO), 1993; Joyce, 1993b; Lee & Burns, 2000; Roberts, 2000).

While it may be argued that change takes time, performance measurement data in state budgeting is not altogether new (Botner, 1985; Brown & Pyers, 1998, Connelly & Tompkins, 1989; Lee, 1991, 1997; Mosso, 1999; NCSL, 1994; Premchand, 1998). Today's reforms are, at least in part, altered and more contemporary forms of previous efforts to bring more systematic analysis of performance into the budget process. Also like past budget reform initiatives, today there exists a large body of literature outlining prescriptions for change and why these changes are needed but little investigation into whether performance budget reform brings about the outcomes envisioned.

The review of the literature on accountability and budgeting permitted the extraction of a variety of reasons that may contribute to the shortcomings of budget process reforms. It raises the issue that in budgeting, administrators are answerable to multiple and diverse accountability demands that constrain administrative discretion. Also, it points out that a number of these constraints are outside the scope of performance budget reform. This chapter discusses the specific questions to be investigated that follow from this literature and describes the research design and specific data collection strategy adopted for their study.

RESEARCH QUESTIONS

It is hypothesized that performance budget reform will not increase administrative discretion in the manner prescriptive theory envisions to the extent that: (1) the implementation of performance budget reform does not bring about the anticipated changes in bureaucratic and political accountability; and (2) legal accountability claims and fiscal constraints, which are beyond the scope of this reform, affect discretion in budgetary decision making.

In this study, administrative discretion means an administrators' ability to exercise his or her own judgement and professional expertise in budgetary decisions. Accountability is understood in terms of its traditional definition of "answerability" however its dimensions are broadened to include current conceptualizations of alternative accountability claims (Dwivedi & Jabbra, 1988; Mansfield, 1982; O'Loughlin, 1990; Romzek & Dubnick, 1987; Waldo, 1982).

Bureaucratic accountability is characterized as a claim that is organizational or administrative (Dwivedi & Jabbra, 1988) where control is exercised by an internal source, typically in the form of a hierarchical structure and rules of operation (Romzek & Dubnick, 1987). Political accountability is characterized as answerability to external actors (O'Loughlin, 1990; Romzek & Dubnick, 1987) which in the budget process, principally focuses on elected officials and central budget staff who have oversight over an administrator's budget request, authorization, and implementation.

Legal accountability is answerability to outside authority in a position to impose legal sanctions or assert formal contractual obligations (O'Loughlin, 1990; Romzek & Dubnick, 1987). Fiscal constraints reflect financial restrictions on the sources and uses of funds due to budgets that are linked to fluctuations in economic conditions by automatic, multiyear spending decisions (i.e. formula funding and indexed appropriations) as well as revenue constraints resulting from both economic cycles and public resistance to higher taxes.

Under the prescriptive theory of performance budget reform, bureaucratic and political accountability systems are expected to change. Governments are to become less bureaucratic and more entrepreneurial, less rule and more mission and results driven. To accomplish this, rules and procedures are to be streamlined and hierarchical controls are to be devolved so that administrators can better respond to both citizens' needs and our fast changing environment.

In exchange for obtaining greater discretion over budgeted resources, administrators commit themselves to specific performance targets (i.e. outputs and outcomes) to result from the implementation of their budgets. In this way, ex ante controls are lessened and accountability maintained by shifting its focus from compliance with rules to responsibility for results.

Bureaucratic Accountability

In terms of bureaucratic accountability, a primary research question is: Do practitioners perceive a reduction in the number of ex ante rules on administrative budget decisions as well as a lessening of red tape with the implementation of performance based budgeting?

Red tape here corresponds to Bozeman's (1993) definition of "formal rules, regulations, and procedures generated by organizational members" that are considered "pathological" (p. 278, 279). This meaning is consistent with popular usage by reform proponents and is similar to that of other scholars (e.g. Kaufman, 1977; Rainey, Pandey & Bozeman, 1995) who identify red tape as the sum of government rules, guidelines, and procedures that are perceived as excessive, duplicative, or pointless.

If reform's proponents are right, practitioners would be expected to perceive change in these restrictions with the advancement of performance budget reform. However, as discussed in the literature, successful remedies for red tape are hard to contrive, for the vast amount of rules, restrictions, and paperwork they inflict individually came about in response to someone's demand for it (Kaufman, 1977; 1996).

Under the category of bureaucratic accountability, it is assumed that the reductions in rules and red tape are those that could be affected by state policy makers and administrators and that are to come about from changes made in the budget process. Yet even with this more limited understanding, it is expected that:

1. The inclusion of performance objectives and results in the budget process is not perceived to lessen budget constraints (rules, regulations, procedures and reporting requirements) that serve as ex ante checks to administrators' budget decisions or to reduce bureaucratic constraints that are perceived as excessive (i.e. red tape).

Along with greater use of performance measurement information in state budgeting, it has been found that agencies nationwide are now subject to more rules, guidelines and compliance requirements by central budget staff in submission of their budget requests (Lee, 1991, 1992, 1997). Congress and state legislators typically have added agency performance data to traditional requirements for their review of the executive budget rather than used this information to substitute for line-item reporting and oversight (Berry, Brower & Flowers, 2000; CBO, 1993; Franklin, Cawley & O'Sullivan-Kachel, 1999; GAO, 1993, 1994; Joyce, 1993a, 1993b; NCSL, 1994). It is therefore expected that at each stage of the budget cycle prior to audit the implementation of performance budget reform:

1.1 Adds (does not substitute) performance measurement information to traditional budget reporting requirement in agency budget requests.

1.2 Increases the number of budget instructions and rules issued by the central budget office for use by agencies in preparing their budget requests.

1.3 Adds (does not substitute) performance measurement information to traditional budget reporting requirements in the executive budget submitted to the legislature for review.

1.4 Does not lessen the number of budget rules, regulations, and procedures agency administrators must comply with in executing their budgets.

Bozeman (1993) has pointed out that it is often not just the number of rules, regulations, and procedures that cause perceptions that they constitute red tape but the "compliance burden" which he defines as the "total resources (time, people, money) actually expended in complying with a rule" (p. 281).

It is not expected that budget practitioners within a state will significantly differ in their perceptions of the change in controls and reporting requirements. However, if as expected, the inclusion of performance budget data in the budget process increases the resources expended in administering the budget process, the perception that these are excessive (i.e. red tape), is more likely to be held by agency administrators than central budget staff.

For this reason the following propositions are posed with respect to red tape:

1.5 The implementation of performance budget reform is perceived to increase significantly the total resources (time, people, and money) expended in administration of the annual/biennial budget process.

1.6 The perception that the total resources (time, people, and money) expended in administration of the annual/biennial budget process is excessive (i.e. red tape) under performance budgeting, is expected to be influenced by the respondent's position.

Political Accountability

Accountability to external political actors is also expected to change which raises the second key question:

2. Does the adoption of performance budgeting bring about a devolution of control from elected officials and central budget staff to program administrators?

The assumption is made under the theory of reform that budget review and appropriation will shift in focus from micromanaging costs toward purchasing results and therefore executive branch budget offices and the legislative body will move away from top-down control of line-items to more flexible forms of budget authorizations.

Administrators are also, in theory, to be given more discretion over how they spend their appropriated funds. This may be done through the use of lump sum appropriations or granting agencies authority to reprogram funds. Some other examples of devolution of control are giving administrators greater flexibility in determining the timing or allotment of funds, the ability to carry over funds from one year to the next, and the capacity to retain within the budget unit some or all of any program savings (Cothran, 1993; Forsythe, 1993; National Commission on the State and Local Public Service, 1993, 1995; Organization for Economic Co-Operation and Development (OECD), 1994, 1995)

Such decentralization of decision making is considered desirable because it brings budgetary decision making closer to the people with knowledge of program needs. Public managers, once freed from rules and red tape, will be able to find more efficient and effective means for accomplishing program goals. Things also move faster if fewer matters have to be referred to the center before they can be resolved allowing administrators to better respond to changing problems and generate budget savings.

However, study of developments in state budgeting over the past twenty years indicate that budget guidance by central budget staff has been shown to be on the increase and that state policy makers and central budget staff have strengthened their control over spending priorities and dollar ceilings (Lee, 1991, 1992, 1997; LeLoup, 1988; Schick, 1990). Moreover, the traditional criticism of budget reform, the political nature of budgetary decisions, has not been countered in today's reform literature.

The results of past reform efforts support Wildvalsky's (1992b) position that politicians cannot be assumed to be "a malleable substance" that will change when faced with more "rational" budget processes (p. 431). Why elected officials will now change their behavior "from emphasizing front-end, micro-level inputs to emphasizing the big picture – the results obtained from public programs" has yet to be convincingly argued by proponents (Joyce, 1993b, p. 13). Contrary to reform's expectations, therefore, it is proposed that:

2.1 The adoption of performance budget reform is not associated with political decision makers or central budget staff granting agency administrators increased flexibility in fund management.

2.2 The adoption of performance budget reform is not perceived to shift significantly the focus of legislative oversight from program costs (i.e. inputs) to program performance (i.e. outputs and outcomes).

2.3 The adoption of performance budget reform does not devolve control from central budget staff to agency administrators, but rather strengthens control of central budget staff and legislators over administrators in the budget process.

While there may be some difference between agency administrators' and central budget staffs' perceptions on changes in political accountability, within a state, these differences are not expected to be significant.

Legal Accountability

Although an administrator's accountability to the law is outside the prescriptions of performance budget reform, the literature of accountability and budgeting indicates its importance. A third question raised in this research is:

3. Do legal accountability claims limit the amount of administrative discretion in budgeting that can be realized from the implementation of performance budget reform?

A program's enabling statutes provide the framework of its decision-making authority, and as Goodsell (1993) points out, while "government should be flexible and innovative . . . government must operate according to the constitution and laws of the land, not niche mission statements" (p. 86). Others (e.g. Frederickson, 1992, 1996; Lowi, 1993; Moe, 1994; Moe & Gilmour, 1995; Peters & Savoie, 1996) voice similar criticisms of current initiatives to reform government that ignore the rule of law.

Specific to budgeting, Straussman (1988) argues that not all budgetary claims are equally protected, and federal, state, and local governments have found that an increasingly larger proportion of their budgets has been "earmarked" for "rights based" programs due to actions taken by the courts (Axelrod, 1989; Bunch & Straussman, 1993; Hackbart & Carson, 1993; LeLoup, 1988). Legal limits, such as those on taxes, expenditures, and debt as well as intergovernmental mandates further limit budgetary discretion in spending. While the significance of legal constraints is expected to vary across programs and states, for practitioners in all areas it is proposed that:

3.1 Laws and the courts' interpretation of them will be perceived as placing significant limits on administrative discretion in budgetary decision making.

3.2 Administrative discretion in budgeting is perceived to be impacted significantly by mandates between levels of government and across branches of government.

Fiscal Constraints

Pressures on public spending in the states have been related to less federal money available, economic conditions, and the public's resistance to higher taxes. While the normative theory of performance budget reform does not address fiscal constraints in terms of prescriptions of change, increased administrative discretion is regarded as a way of generating budget savings by allowing more innovative and entrepreneurial decisions and it is often considered a trade-off to cushion the effects of cuts (Cochran, 1993; Grey, Jenkins & Segworth, 1993; Frederickson, 1996; Kettl, 2000; Radin, 2000; Schick, 1990). A fourth question of this inquiry is:

4. Do fiscal constraints restrict the exercise of an administrator's own judgment in determining program spending?

The current literature on budgeting demonstrates that multiyear spending decisions built into the structure of many programs, particularly entitlements and other formula funded programs have heightened the sensitivity of the budget to changes in growth rates, inflation, and unemployment. A consequence has been the need to shift the burden of funding and/or provision of other public services through the use of enterprise funds, contracting out, user fees, and an array of other mechanisms to increase alternative funding sources or shrink the number of services government provides. These various sources of funds and service arrangements restrict administrative flexibility in budgeting decisions.

Furthermore, fiscal constraints narrow the choices available to public managers and reenforce an emphasis on top-down spending controls (Dupont-Morales & Harris, 1994; Marlowe & Arrington, 1994; LeLoup, 1988; Wilson & Sylvia, 1993). While the extent of restriction imposed by fiscal constraints is expected to vary across programs and states. for practitioners in all areas it is proposed that:

4.1 Fiscal constraints on budgets due to less money available are perceived as significant limits to the exercise of an administrator's own judgment in program spending.

4.2 Fiscal constraints on budgets due to less discretion in spending the funds that are available (e.g. multiyear expenditures, earmarked funds, compulsory statewide adjustments) are perceived as significant limits to the exercise of an administrator's own judgment in program spending.

Administrative Discretion

While each of the previous questions addresses particular accountability claims and constraints identified in the literature, the overarching research question of this study is:

5. Does performance budget reform increase the discretion of administrators in budgetary decision making?

Based upon the theoretical rationales drawn from the literature and cited above, it is expected that:

5.1 Practitioners will not perceive that the implementation of performance budget reform increases their administrative discretion.

In sum, no significant increase in overall perceptions of administrative discretion is expected regardless of how well developed the performance budgeting process is in a state.

MEASUREMENT STRATEGY FOR PRINCIPAL CONCEPTS

Administrative Discretion

Using a self-administered questionnaire, the study asks practitioners to assess whether they perceive that the use of performance measures and standards in budgeting brings about administrative discretion at the present time. Responses are measured on a Likert-type scale and are sought as to perceptions of an administrator's overall ability to base budget decisions on his or her judgement and professional expertise and whether they perceive that accountability in budgeting has changed from compliance with rules to accountability for results.

Practitioners are also asked to indicate their perception of the importance of the following factors to administrative discretion in budgeting, also measured on a Likert-type scale: reduction in administrative rules, shift in political decision makers' oversight focus, and changes in laws and fiscal constraints.

Rules and Red Tape

Practitioners' perceptions regarding reduction in rules, procedures, and guidelines will be measured with single-item questions asking respondents to indicate their agreement or disagreement with statements about the amount or number of these constraints. Responses will be sought in three stages of the budget cycle where ex ante controls are expected to be reduced: budget requests, budget review, and budget execution.

Most red tape studies (e.g. Baldwin, 1990; Bozeman & Loveless, 1987; Buchanan, 1975; Rosenfeld, 1984) have measured the concept similarly to this type of questionnaire item. However, recent studies also have measured red tape based on procedural delays or the amount of time taken to complete administrative tasks (e.g. Bozeman, 1993; Bozeman, Reed & Scott, 1992; Lan & Rainey, 1992), sometimes with different results (Bozeman, 1993, p. 330). For this reason, the survey will also measure practitioners' assessment of the time and resources that they devote to the collection and monitoring of performance measurement data in the budget process.

Decentralization and Devolution of Control

Questions to measure devolution of control will examine at what level in the organization budgetary decisions can formally be made. Respondents will be asked to indicate their agreement or disagreement with statements about decisions regarding: (1) reprogramming funds, (2) the timing or allotment of funds, and (3) the retention of surplus program funds. Questionnaire items also will use Likert-type scales to measure practitioners' perceptions of change in the focus of oversight by legislators in terms of whether they perceived a shift away from detailed itemization of appropriations toward performance and increased control awarded to administrators.

Legal Constraints

The significance of legal constraints will be measured by asking respondents to what degree they perceive that a program's enabling statutes limit discretion in budgetary decisions. The percentage of the current fiscal year's total budget determined by court decisions, intergovernmental mandates, and constitutionally dedicated sources will also be requested and used to measure their impact on discretion in spending.

Fiscal Constraints

Practitioners will be asked how strongly they agree or disagree with statements regarding whether: (1) the predominant impact of fewer funds available is to restrict administrative discretion in budgeting decisions; (2) alternative means of financing limit the exercise of an administrator's professional judgement on program spending; (3) compulsory adjustments common to all state agencies limit the flexibility they have in their program's budget decisions; and (4) multiyear, automatic funding decisions significantly restrict administrative discretion in budget decision making.

Background Characteristics

Respondents will be asked to provide the number of years they have been in the current position and in the current organization. They will also be asked the size of their program area measured in current dollar outlays and full time personnel.

OVERALL RESEARCH DESIGN

A principal purpose of the research is to expand existing knowledge about performance budget reform in the states and to ask practitioners about their perceptions of its effects. In particular, interest centers on the extent to which this reform is perceived to promote additional discretion for budget administrators and whether alternative accountability claims and constraints explain expected differences between practitioners' perceptions and reformers' predictions. To accomplish the assessment of performance budgeting impacts within a cross-sectional design, the budget process and use of performance measures in each state were first examined.

Although most states report using performance measurement data in their budget process, it is important to acknowledge that the forms and the stage or progress in implementing performance budget reform differ (Jordan & Hackbart, 1999; Lee, 1991; 1997; Lee & Burns, 2000; Melkers, & Willoughby, 1998; Willoughby & Melkers, 2000). For the purposes of this study, performance budget reforms are considered those which:

(1) Constitute an identifiable ongoing program or formal initiative charged with the task of integrating performance measures including inputs, outputs, and outcomes into the state budget process.
(2) Are directed or coordinated by a unit located in the central administration or reporting to the governor or other official of the central administration or legislature, and
(3) Are extended to select, if not all operating agencies, in a uniform manner.

This definition is similar to that adopted by Poister, Hatry, Fisk and Greiner (1985) in examining diverse productivity improvement efforts in state government. It allows for a variety of approaches to performance budget reform; however, requires that outcomes measures of performance be included in reform efforts and emphasizes centralized efforts in contrast with ad hoc performance budgeting initiatives that individual agencies take on their own initiative.

The study population is agency administrators and central budget staff in all states in program areas of Education K-12, Corrections, and Revenue. To determine the status of reform initiatives in each state, descriptive data were collected from secondary sources, then sent to all fifty state executive budget offices to be updated and supplemented so that it reflected the current status as of July, 1996.

Using these same data, states were classified into six groups ranked according to the level of sophistication of their performance budgeting process. To rank the states, a seven-item scale was constructed based upon: (1) the scope of reform (no reform – 0, pilot programs only – 1, phase-in of all agencies/ programs – 2, all agencies/programs – 3); (2) the length of time reform has been implemented (not implemented – 0; less than a complete budget cycle for agencies being phased in or only pilots in effect – 1, one or more budget cycles for agencies phased in or less than one budget cycle for all agencies – 2, one or two budget cycle(s) for all agencies – 3, three or more budget cycles for all agencies – 4); (3) how performance measures are reported (not reported – 0, in a separate report or supplement to the budget – 1, in the budget document – 2); (4) who verifies performance measurement data (not verified – 0, agency only – 1, central executive budget staff – 2, central legislative budget staff – 3, state auditor – 4); (5) extent of training of central executive budget staff on performance measurement and monitoring (no training – 0, one year – 1, two or more years – 2); (6) extent of training of agency administrators on performance measurement and monitoring (no training – 0, one year – 1, two or more years – 2); and (7) the state of integration of budgeting, accounting, and performance information systems (not yet addressed – 0, under development by individual agencies – 1, under development as a centralized management information system – 2, available in individual agencies – 3, available in a centralized management information system – 4). Thus, the range of possible scores is from 0 (no reform) to a high score of 21.

This scale is based upon prior reviews of performance budgeting initiatives. The U.S. General Accounting Office (GAO) (1993) selected states as "leaders" in performance budgeting for the following reasons: (1) each regularly published performance measures in its budget documents; (2) each reported using a variety of measures, including outcome and output productivity measures and, (3) each reported using performance measures through at least two budget cycles.

In their study, the GAO reported that a reason why performance measurement data were not used in budget deliberations by state legislators was the fact that measures had not been verified either by legislative staff or state auditors. Brown and Pyers (1998) and Mosso (1999) identify audits as key elements in developing an effective performance-based management system. OECD (1995, p. 54) similarly considered the auditing of performance measurement data as an indicator of further advancement toward budgeting for results.

The scope of performance reform in terms of pilot projects, phase-in of programs or general implementation is also identified by OECD (1994, pp. 29–30) as a means to distinguish initiatives. Whether performance measures are, or are not, reported in various budget documents is used by researchers to evaluate state budget reforms (e.g. Florida Office of Program Policy Analysis and Government Accountability, 1997; Jordon & Hackbart, 1999; Lee & Burns, 2000; NASBO, 1990, 1995, 1997). Training and information management systems have been cited as vital elements of performance-based reforms by both scholars and practitioners in public budgeting (e.g. Axelrod, 1989; Curro, 1995; Grey, Jenkins & Segsworth, 1993; Greiner, 1996; Forsythe, 1993; Howard, 1973; Lee, 1991, 1992, 1997; Louisiana Office of Planning & Budget, 1996; Minnesota Department of Finance, 1996; Mosso, 1999; National Commission on the State and Local Public Service, 1995; Virginia Department of Planning & Budget, 1996).

After assessing the development of states' reform initiatives, the study sought practitioners' views on performance budget reform, discretion and alternative accountability claims. For this reason individuals, who supply information on actual state practice or their perceptions of state practice, were the unit of analysis. Their responses to questionnaire items were examined to see if they perceived a positive relationship between the implementation of reform and administrative discretion.

DATA COLLECTION PLAN

There is a series of milestones accomplished in the study design: (1) background information is collected on budget practices in each state; (2) questions that operationalize the variables in the research questions are assembled into a questionnaire; (3) the questionnaire (and scales) are pretested; and (4) a self-administered version of the revised questionnaire is mailed to a census of respondents. As mentioned above, the data for this study are assembled in two phases. First, data on the implementation status of performance budget reform in each state were collected and ranked by the researcher. The second phase assembled information on practitioners' perceptions concerning the adoption of performance budgeting and administrative discretion.

Because the implementation of performance budget reform varies across the states and these practices are changing continuously, the descriptions of performance measurement practices gathered from secondary sources were sent to state budget officers for verification and updating. Additional information describing their reform effort to date was also requested which could not be found from available reports.

In July 1996, all fifty state budget offices were polled concerning their budget process and use of performance measures. This information was requested from the budget official identified as responsible for performance measurement as listed in the *Directory of State Budget Officers* (NASBO, 1995). These state budget officials first were contacted by telephone to determine if this information could be exchanged via email over the internet. In total, fourteen states were able to exchange information in this way. A personalized letter, list of questions, and stamped, self-addressed, return envelope were mailed to the other thirty-six states (See Appendix A).

The second stage of data collection required the development of a questionnaire for practitioners. A self-administered questionnaire was mailed to agency administrators and central budget staff in August 1996. Respondents in program areas of Education K-12, Corrections and Revenue were surveyed in every state (see Appendix B).

As mentioned in Chapter One, because of the proportion of resources allocated to education and its perceived importance to citizens and elected officials, Education K-12 was among the first program areas focused on for the application of performance measures (GASB, 1990). Corrections is one of the fastest growing program areas in state spending. Revenue departments serve key functions in state budgeting and represent a different type of program area. Another decision criterion for selection was that, to the degree possible, the institutional level (and organizational layers) be essentially consistent across states. Each of these program areas typically comprise an independent agency or department in all state governments.

Seeking responses from two different groups offers different frames of reference. Agency administrators are especially knowledgeable of program activities, statutory mandates and other programmatic information which may affect discretion. However, central budget offices typically engage in revenue forecasting activities, oversight and management of spending across all programs of state government, affording analysts a better understanding of political and fiscal constraints.

Because there are two different questionnaire recipients, there are two different frames or listing of potential participants. The State Yellow Book (Monitor Publishing, 1996) was used as the source of the names and addresses of agency administrators. The Directory of State Budget Officers (NASBO, 1995) provided the names and addresses of central budget staff and the program area over which they have responsibility.

The procedure for administering the mailed questionnaire follows the process to generate high levels of questionnaire completion used by survey researchers (Babbie, 1990). The questionnaire, explanatory cover letter and a self-addressed, stamped envelope were mailed to the individuals included in the survey. After ten days, each person who did not respond was contacted by telephone and an additional questionnaire faxed if necessary. Ten days after the second contact, a letter was mailed to non-respondents again asking for their cooperation, enclosing another questionnaire and explaining that a follow-up call would be made.

V. BUDGETING IN THE STATES: STUDY RESULTS

This chapter presents the profiles of the survey respondents and the results of the data analyses. Interpretations of the data are organized by the five research questions introduced in the previous chapter. More extensive comments about the implications of the research findings and suggestions for further research are reserved for the next chapter.

PROFILE OF RESPONDENTS

The overall response rate for the survey was 63%. While there are no established completion guidelines for censuses (Wallach, 1977), this response rate was higher than expected. A lower response rate was anticipated because agency-central budget office budget preparations were underway in many states and potentially disinterested individuals from out-of-state were surveyed. However, follow-up procedures to encourage questionnaire completion was believed to have contributed to greater participation in the survey.

Of the 299 questionnaires sent out, 187 were returned, 51% by agency administrators and 49% by budget office analysts. This corresponds to the proportion of questionnaires mailed to each group. Among those who did not participate in the survey, thirty-two responded that they would not or could not, either in writing or over the phone.[1] Table 3 shows that the responses received were evenly distributed across the program areas studied.

Table 3. Number and Percentage of Survey Responses by Program Area.

Program Area	Number contacted	Number of responses	Percentage of responses
Corrections	100	65	65%
Revenue	99	54	55%
Education K-12	100	68	68%
All Programs	299	187	63%

Table 4. Response Rate by Geographic Region and Organizational Size.

Geographical region	Number contacted	Number of responses	Percentage of responses
Northeast (1)	54	27	50%
South (2)	98	71	72%
Midwest (3)	72	45	63%
West (4)	75	44	59%
Organizational Size (fiscal year 1997 full time equivalent positions (FTES) authorized)			
86 to 400 FTES	71	45	63%
401 to 1000 FTES	75	48	64%
1001 to 3000 FTES	85	47	55%
Over 3,000 FTES	68	47	69%

The organizations studied were categorized by geographic regions as established by the United States Bureau of the Census, and organizational size, based on Fiscal Year 1997 full time equivalent positions authorized (FTES) for the state agencies. Information on FTES was requested on the survey instrument and was collected from non-participating states by telephone. This allowed responses to be monitored to help detect apparent systematic bias in participation (Babbie, 1990).

Table 4 presents the breakdown of survey responses by these categories which shows that, while there was a higher response rate from states in the South, all geographic regions and the full range of sizes of organizations were represented.

Of the 95 respondents from state agencies 28 (30%) held the top position of secretary, commissioner, or director of the agency, 58 (61%) were deputy or assistant commissioners or directors in charge of administration, finance or budgeting for the agency, 9 (9%) held other positions. The 92 respondents from central executive budget offices were not classified according to position because job titles were difficult to compare across states. Some states use "senior analyst" while others designate seniority by numerals (i.e. Budget Analyst IV) or other terms such as "program supervisor". However, as illustrated in Table 5, budget analysts reported on average six years in their

Table 5. Respondents' Years in Current Position, Years in Current Organization and Years in State Government.

Respondent	Years in current position		Years in current organization		Years in state government	
	mean	mode	mean	mode	mean	mode
Agency commissioner or director	3	2	8	1	14	5, 10, 18*
Agency deputy commissioner	6	1	13	2 & 3**	18	22
Agency administrator	4	5	7	4	13	24
Central executive budget officer	6	1	10	4	14	10 & 21**

* multiple modes; ** bimodal.

current position and even longer tenure with their organization, indicating they were experienced in their jobs.

The average number of years respondents had been in their current positions ranged from three to six years. Most respondents reported being in their current position for one to five years. Since top administrators of state agencies typically experience turnover with a change in administrations, a three year term in the position does not seem unusual, particularly in this, an election year. Respondents reported being in their current organization and in state government for much longer periods of time with the mean number of years in their organization ranging from seven to thirteen years, and in state government from fourteen to eighteen years.

The number of years most frequently reported for experience in state government was surprisingly high. For agency administrators this may be in part due to the fact that corrections, education, and revenue are fairly specialized program areas that require experience and knowledge in the field. Budget analysts over these program areas may have such long tenure in their organizations for this same reason. Also, revenue departments serve a critical function in funding state government, while education and corrections are among the largest and fastest growing spending areas in most states and, therefore, typically are reviewed by senior staff. These statistics, in sum, do indicate that respondents have a significant experience level to draw upon in answering the questions posed here.

PERFORMANCE BUDGET REFORM ISSUES

As discussed in the previous chapter, it is hypothesized that performance budget reform may not increase administrative discretion in the manner prescriptive theory envisions to the extent that: (1) the implementation of performance budget reform does not bring about expected changes in political and bureaucratic accountability; and (2) legal accountability claims and fiscal constraints, which are beyond the scope of this reform, affect discretion in budgetary decision making.

Practitioners' responses to questions regarding legal accountability claims and fiscal constraints were not expected to be related to the implementation of reform. However, it was proposed that if reform's proponents are correct, practitioners would be expected to perceive change in political and bureaucratic accountability claims with the advancement of performance budget reform.

Bureaucratic Accountability

1. Do practitioners perceive a reduction in the number of ex ante rules on administrative budget decisions as well as a lessening of red tape with the implementation of performance based budgeting?

Under-performance budget reform, bureaucratic constraints in the budget process are to be reduced as accountability shifts from compliance with rules toward responsibility for results. Yet, contrary to predictions of reformers, it was expected that the inclusion of performance objectives and results in the budget process would not be perceived to lessen rules, regulations, procedures and reporting requirements that serve as ex ante checks to administrators' budget decisions.

Tables 6 through 11 show the extent to which respondents agreed or disagreed with a series of four statements that reflected changes in the number of ex ante rules at different stages in the budget cycle. Six respondent groups represent the different levels of advancement in implementing budget reform. As illustrated in Table 6, respondents at all stages of reform agreed (overall mean = 3.1) that top down rules and instructions used in the preparing an

Table 6. Level of Agreement That Performance Budget Reform Increases Budget Instructions and Rules In Budget Preparation, Difference by Group.

Source	D.F.	Analysis of Variance Sum of Squares	Mean Squares	*F* Ratio	*F* Prob.
Between Groups	5	4.6062	0.9212	0.5983	0.7013
Within Groups	143	220.1992	1.5399		
			Mean[a]	Std Dev	N[b]
For Entire Population			3.1678	1.2325	149
GROUP 1 Very advanced			3.5556	1.1304	9
GROUP 2 More advanced			2.8947	1.4101	19
GROUP 3 Somewhat advanced			3.2500	1.4222	12
GROUP 4 Not too advanced			3.2500	1.1794	56
GROUP 5 Preliminary stage			3.0000	1.1785	37
GROUP 6 No reform			3.3125	1.3022	16

[a] Scale for response: Strongly agree = 1, More than agree = 2, Agree = 3, Neutral = 4, Disagree = 5, More than disagree = 6, Strongly disagree = 7.

[b] Number of responses indicating performance measures not used (37). Number of missing observations (1).

Table 7. Level of Agreement That Performance Budget Reform Increases Budget Instructions and Rules In Budget Preparation, Difference by Group and Organization.

Source		Sum of D.F.	Analysis of Variance Mean Squares	*F* Squares	*F* Ratio	Prob.
Main Effects						
GROUP		5	4.628	0.926	0.595	0.704
ORG		1	0.027	0.027	0.017	0.895
2-way Interactions						
GROUP	ORG	5	6.869	1.374	0.882	0.495
			Mean[a] Budget Office	Std Dev Budget Office	Mean Agency	Std Dev Agency
For Entire Population			3.1733	1.2122	3.1622	1.2609
GROUP 1 Very advanced			4.0000	0.8165	3.2000	1.3038
GROUP 2 More advanced			2.6364	1.1202	3.2500	1.7525
GROUP 3 Somewhat advanced			3.2857	1.2536	3.2000	1.7889
GROUP 4 Not too advanced			3.3929	1.2274	3.1071	1.3333
GROUP 5 Preliminary stage			2.7778	1.1144	3.2105	1.2283
GROUP 6 NO reform			3.5714	1.3973	3.1111	1.2693

[a] Scale for response: Strongly agree = 1, More than agree = 2, Agree = 3, Neutral = 4, Disagree = 5, More than disagree = 6, Strongly disagree = 7.

agency's budget request *increased* with the implementation of reform ($F = 0.60$, $p > 0.05$).

Table 7 suggests that the organizational perspective of the respondent does not substantially change this opinion. Except for a very small number of central budget office analysts in the most advanced group who are neutral, on average, all agency administrators and budget analysts, whose offices promulgate these rules, agreed that budget guidance and the number of rules increased. Thus the main effects for organizational perspective ("ORG") and the level of implementing budget reform ("GROUP") are not statistically significant ($p > 0.05$); the interaction effects are also not statistically significant.

Table 8 summarizes practitioners responses to two statements regarding reporting requirements. Both in agencies' budget requests and in the executive budget submitted to the legislature, performance measurement information was perceived to add to, not be a substitute for, traditional line-item reporting at all stages of reform. As illustrated, the average score indicated agreement, with no statistically significant differences across groups at different stages in implementing reform ($F = 1.26$, $p > 0.05$).

Table 9 expands this analysis to take into account whether the respondents were agency administrators or central budget office analysts. These data show that perceptions did not significantly vary according to respondent's organization ($F = 0.124$, $p > 0.05$) nor were they found to change when controlled for the size of organization.

Tables 10 and 11 show responses to a statement that was phrased in accordance with the position of reformers. It claimed that reporting performance measures and standards in the budget process reduced the number of budget rules, regulations, and procedures agency administrators must comply with in executing their budget. Consistent with responses to earlier questions, three of the six respondent groups disagreed (mean > 5) while two other groups were slightly more neutral having means of 4.89 and 4.87. Ultimately, none of these means were statistically significantly different across groups representing differing levels in implementing reform ($F = 1.72$, $p > 0.05$).

Interestingly, as shown in Table 11, budget analysts were, on average, slightly more opposed to this statement than agency practitioners. This was most pronounced in the opinions of respondents in the most advanced states. Even so, organizational perspective as an agency administrator or central budget office analyst did not show a statistically significant main effect ($F = 0.79$, $p > 0.05$).

While an objective was to explore the relationship between the stage of reform and perceptions of bureaucratic constraints, the relationship between

Table 8. Level of Agreement That Performance Budget Reform Adds to Traditional Reporting Requirements, Difference By Group.

Source	D.F.	Analysis of Variance Sum of Squares	Mean Squares	*F* Ratio	*F* Prob.
Between Groups	5	11.0870	2.2174	1.2679	0.2811
Within Groups	142	248.3387	1.7489		
			Mean[a]	Std Dev	N[b]
For Entire Population			2.8446	1.3285	148
GROUP 1 Very advanced			3.3333	1.1180	9
GROUP 2 More advanced			2.5789	1.3045	19
GROUP 3 Somewhat advanced			2.1667	0.9374	12
GROUP 4 Not too advanced			3.0364	1.3189	55
GROUP 5 Preliminary stage			2.8108	1.4306	37
GROUP 6 No reform			2.8125	1.4245	16

[a] Scale for response: Strongly agree = 1, More than agree = 2, Agree = 3, Neutral = 4, Disagree = 5, More than disagree = 6, Strongly disagree = 7.
[b] Number of responses indicating performance measures not used (37). Number of missing observations (2).

Table 9. Level of Agreement That Performance Budget Reform Adds to Traditional Reporting Requirements, Difference By Group and Organization.

Source		D.F.	Analysis of Variance Sum of Squares	Mean Squares	*F* Ratio	*F* Prob.
Main Effects						
GROUP		5	11.250	2.250	1.244	0.292
ORG		1	0.224	0.224	0.124	0.725
2-way Interactions						
GROUP	ORG	5	2.147	0.429	0.237	0.945
			Mean[a] Budget Office	Std Dev Budget Office	Mean Agency	Std Dev Agency
For Entire Population			2.8649	1.2532	2.8243	1.4080
GROUP 1 Very advanced			3.2500	1.2583	3.4000	1.1402
GROUP 2 More advanced			2.5455	1.1282	3.2500	1.5980
GROUP 3 Somewhat advanced			2.2857	0.9512	3.2000	1.0000
GROUP 4 Not too advanced			3.0741	1.3280	3.1071	1.3333
GROUP 5 Preliminary stage			3.0000	1.4951	3.2105	1.3829
GROUP 6 No reform			2.5714	0.5345	3.1111	1.8708

[a] Scale for response: Strongly agree = 1, More than agree = 2, Agree = 3, Neutral = 4, Disagree = 5, More than disagree = 6, Strongly disagree = 7.

Table 10. Level of Agreement That Performance Budget Reform Reduces Rules, Regulations and Reporting Requirements In Agency Execution of Budget, Difference By Group.

Source	D.F.	Analysis of Variance Sum of Squares	Mean Squares	*F* Ratio	*F* Prob.
Between Groups	5	16.3132	3.2626	1.7257	0.1324
Within Groups	143	270.3579	1.8906		
			Mean[a]	Std Dev	N[b]
For Entire Population			5.0470	1.3917	149
GROUP 1 Very advanced			4.1111	1.1667	9
GROUP 2 More advanced			5.1579	1.5728	19
GROUP 3 Somewhat advanced			5.4167	1.0836	12
GROUP 4 Not too advanced			4.8929	1.3575	56
GROUP 5 Preliminary stage			5.4054	1.2793	37
GROUP 6 No reform			4.8750	1.6683	16

[a] Scale for response: Strongly agree = 1, More than agree = 2, Agree = 3, Neutral = 4, Disagree = 5, More than disagree = 6, Strongly disagree = 7.
[b] Number of responses indicating performance measures not used (37). Number of missing observations (1).

Table 11. Level of Agreement That Performance Budget Reform Reduces Rules, Regulations and Reporting Requirement In Agency Execution of Budget, Difference By Group and Organization.

Source		D.F.	Analysis of Variance Sum of Squares	Mean Squares	*F* Ratio	*F* Prob.
Main Effects						
GROUP		5	15.898	3.180	1.673	0.145
ORG		1	1.514	1.514	0.797	0.374
2-way Interactions						
GROUP	ORG	5	8.537	1.707	0.899	0.484
			Mean[a] Budget Office	Std Dev Budget Office	Mean Agency	Std Dev Agency
For Entire Population			5.1600	1.3759	4.9324	1.4077
GROUP 1 Very advanced			4.5000	1.2910	3.8000	1.0954
GROUP 2 More advanced			5.4545	1.5076	4.7500	1.6690
GROUP 3 Somewhat advanced			5.2285	0.9512	5.6000	1.3416
GROUP 4 Not too advanced			4.8214	1.3892	4.9643	1.3467
GROUP 5 Preliminary stage			5.4444	1.5038	5.3684	1.0651
GROUP 6 No reform			5.5714	1.1339	4.3333	1.8708

[a] Scale for response: Strongly agree = 1, More than agree = 2, Agree = 3, Neutral = 4, Disagree = 5, More than disagree = 6, Strongly disagree = 7.

these two variables was not found to be statistically significant because so large a proportion of respondents at every stage in implementing reform held similar opinions. In contrast to the prediction of reform advocates, respondents on average did not feel strongly (agree or strongly agree) that bureaucratic constraints were streamlined with the implementation of reform. To the contrary, respondents averaged strong opinions (agreed/strongly agreed) that with the reporting of performance measures and standards in budgeting, bureaucratic constraints were increased.

This finding probably should not be surprising. Rules and regulations can proliferate at various stages of the process and not necessarily be stratified according to reform's development. For example, rules are numerous at the early stages of reform to establish the process as well as at later stages when greater breadth of coverage, sophistication of performance measurement and their monitoring give rise to other, often more technical rules and regulations.

It was expected that, if the inclusion of performance measurement data in budgeting increased the resources (time, people, and money) expended in administering the budget process, the perception that these administrative requirements are excessive (i.e. red tape) was more likely to be held by agency administrators than central budget staff. As shown in Table 12, respondents on average tended to agree (overall mean = 3.6) that implementing performance budget reform increased the resources (time, people, and money) expended. The mean score was also in the "agree" range with no statistically significant differences by degree of budget reform ($F = 0.10$, $p > 0.05$) or by organizational perspective ($F = 0.63$, $p > 0.05$). Even so practitioners were less of the opinion that this was too much.

Table 13 shows mean levels of agreement to the claim that the reporting of performance measures and standards requires that "too much time, people and money be dedicated to administration of the annual/biennial budget process". In these data the means were in the neutral to disagree range, with no statistically significant differences by organizational perspective ($F = 1.64$, $p > 0.05$) or by degree of budget reform ($F = 1.11$, $p > 0.05$). Consequently, while reform is perceived to increase the resources expended in administration, on average, it is not considered to be excessive by either agency administrators or central budget staff.

Political Accountability

2. Does the adoption of performance budgeting bring about a devolution of control from elected officials and central budget staff to program administrators?

Table 12. Level of Agreement That Performance Budget Reform Increases the Resources Expended On Administration of the Budget Process, Difference by Group and Organization.

Source		D.F.	Analysis of Variance Sum of Squares	Mean Squares	*F* Ratio	*F* Prob.
Main Effects						
GROUP		5	1.127	0.225	0.101	0.992
ORG		1	1.408	1.408	0.633	0.428
2-way Interactions						
GROUP	ORG	5	2.007	0.401	0.181	0.970
			Mean[a] Budget Office	Std Dev Budget Office	Mean Agency	Std Dev Agency
For Entire Population			3.6027	1.3201	3.4054	1.5608
GROUP 1 Very advanced			3.6670	0.5775	3.4000	0.8944
GROUP 2 More advanced			3.8000	1.5492	3.3750	1.8468
GROUP 3 Somewhat advanced			3.2857	0.3801	3.4000	1.8166
GROUP 4 Not too advanced			3.7500	1.2360	3.3929	1.7499
GROUP 5 Preliminary stage			3.3889	1.4200	3.5263	1.5044
GROUP 6 No reform			3.5714	1.5119	3.2222	1.3017

[a] Scale for response: Strongly agree = 1, More than agree = 2, Agree = 3, Neutral = 4, Disagree = 5, More than disagree = 6, Strongly disagree = 7.

Table 13. Level of Agreement That Performance Budget Reform Requires Too Many Resources Be Expended In Administration of the Budget Process, Difference By Group and Organization.

Source		D.F.	Analysis of Variance Sum of Squares	Mean Squares	*F* Ratio	*F* Prob.
Main Effects						
GROUP		5	12.121	2.424	1.113	0.356
ORG	1	3.579	3.579	1.644	0.202	
2-way Interactions						
GROUP	ORG	5	1.506	0.301	0.138	0.983
			Mean[a] Budget Office	Std Dev Budget Office	Mean Agency	Std Dev Agency
For Entire Population			4.4595	1.3158	4.1486	1.5849
GROUP 1 Very advanced			4.3333	1.1547	4.6000	0.5477
GROUP 2 More advanced			4.5455	1.5076	4.1250	1.8077
GROUP 3 Somewhat advanced			4.1429	0.6901	3.6000	1.9494
GROUP 4 Not too advanced			4.8214	1.3068	4.3929	1.8726
GROUP 5 Preliminary stage			4.2222	1.4371	3.9474	1.3529
GROUP 6 No reform			3.8571	1.2150	3.8889	1.1667

[a] Scale for response: Strongly agree = 1, More than agree = 2, Agree = 3, Neutral = 4, Disagree = 5, More than disagree = 6, Strongly disagree = 7.

In contrast to the prescriptive theory of performance budget reform, it was proposed that with the advancement of reform, political decision makers would not grant administrators greater discretion in fund management nor would legislative oversight be perceived to have shifted from dollar inputs or program costs toward the broader view, results achieved. Instead, control by legislators and central budget staff over administrators was expected to be perceived to be strengthened.

Discretion in Fund Management

Table 14 indicates that respondents from the states most advanced in implementing performance budget reform (Group 1) did perceive a change in fund management as prescribed by reform's proponents ($F = 4.57$, $p < 0.01$). Respondents from these states, on average, agreed that the legislature used more flexible funding formats (e.g. lump sum appropriations) giving administrators more discretion in budget execution. A second statement, which claimed that reporting performance measures in the budget process had resulted in less itemization and detailed instructions in budget appropriations, corroborated this finding. As shown in Table 15, respondents from the states most advanced in implementing reform agreed, but to a lesser extent, that itemization in appropriations was reduced ($F = 2.71$, $p < 0.05$). The mean score for Group 1 indicated overall agreement with this claim (mean = 3.5), whereas all groups less advanced in implementing budget reform registered means in the disagree range (5.0 through 5.5).

In response to two other questionnaire items regarding relaxation of control over agency transfers of funds and more administrative discretion over the allotment of funds there were no statistically significant differences between groups at different levels of implementing reform. As shown in Table 16, respondents from Group 1 agreed (mean = 3.4) while respondents from states that were at a lesser stage of development were neutral or disagreed (mean range 4.4 through 5.1) that there had been a reduction of control over an agency's discretion in fund transfers. Because of the small number of cases in the "very advanced" group, the difference – while substantively notable – is not large enough to be statistically significant (Blalock, 1979, p. 319).

Table 17 presents a similar pattern of means across groups with respect to increased discretion in the timing of funds. The most advanced group tended to agree (mean = 3.78) that discretion over the allotment of funds increased, whereas respondents from states at lower levels of reform were neutral or disagreed (mean range from 4.6 through 5.0). Though substantively interesting,

Table 14. Level of Agreement That Reporting Performance Measures and Standards Increases Flexibility in the Format of Appropriations, Difference By Group.

Source	D.F.	Analysis of Variance Sum of Squares	Mean Squares	*F* Ratio	*F* Prob.
Between Groups	5	53.1757	10.6351	4.5704	0.0007
Within Groups	137	318.7963	2.3270		
		Group 1	Mean[a]	Std Dev	N[b]
For Entire Population			4.8322	1.6185	143
GROUP 1.0 very advanced			2.7778	0.9718	9
GROUP 2.0 more advanced			4.2941	1.8291	17
GROUP 3.0 somewhat advanced		*	5.2727	1.4206	11
GROUP 4.0 not too advanced		*	5.0370	1.5167	54
GROUP 5.0 preliminary stage		*	5.2162	1.4932	37
GROUP 6.0 no reform		*	4.6667	1.5887	15

[a] Scale for response: Strongly agree = 1, More than agree = 2, Agree = 3, Neutral = 4, Disagree = 5, More than disagree = 6, Strongly disagree = 7.
[b] Number of responses indicating performance measures not used (37). Number of missing observations (7).
* Denotes pairs of groups significantly different at the 0.01 level.

Table 15. Level of Agreement That Reporting Performance Measures and Standards Lessens Itemization In Budget Appropriations.

Source	D.F.	Analysis of Variance Sum of Squares	Mean Squares	*F* Ratio	*F* Prob.
Between Groups	5	26.9689	5.3938	2.7155	0.0224
Within Groups	142	282.0582	1.9863		
		Group 1	Mean[a]	Std Dev	N[b]
For Entire Population			5.0811	1.4499	148
GROUP 1 Very advanced			3.5556	1.5092	9
GROUP 2 More advanced		*	5.4211	1.5390	19
GROUP 3 Somewhat advanced		*	5.5000	1.1677	12
GROUP 4 Not too advanced		*	5.0179	1.4205	56
GROUP 5 Preliminary stage		*	5.2778	1.4265	36
GROUP 6 No reform		*	5.0000	1.2649	16

[a] Scale for response: Strongly agree = 1, More than agree = 2, Agree = 3, Neutral = 4, Disagree = 5, More than disagree = 6, Strongly disagree = 7.
[b] Number of responses indicating performance measures not used (37). Number of missing observations (2).
* Denotes pairs of groups significantly different at the 0.050 level.

Table 16. Level of Agreement That Reporting of Performance Measures and Standards Increases Administration Discretion To Transfer Funds, Difference by Group.

		Analysis of Variance			
Source	D.F.	Sum of Squares	Mean Squares	*F* Ratio	*F* Prob.
Between Groups	5	22.1966	4.4393	1.8490	0.1073
Within Groups	137	328.9223	2.4009		
			Mean[a]	Std Dev	N[b]
For Entire Population			4.7972	1.5725	143
GROUP 1 Very advanced			3.3750	1.1877	8
GROUP 2 More advanced			4.4444	2.0065	18
GROUP 3 Somewhat advanced			4.9091	1.3003	11
GROUP 4 Not too advanced			4.9074	1.4310	54
GROUP 5 Preliminary stage			5.0811	1.6895	37
GROUP 6 No reform			4.8000	1.2649	15

[a] Scale for response: Strongly agree = 1, More than agree = 2, Agree = 3, Neutral = 4, Disagree = 5, More than disagree = 6, Strongly disagree = 7.

[b] Number of responses indicating performance measures not used (37). Number of missing observations (7).

these differences were not great enough to be statistically significant ($F = 1.19$, $p > 0.05$).

Oversight Focus on Results

Table 18 shows that on average most respondents were neutral regarding the claim that performance budgeting shifts political decision makers' oversight focus toward results (overall mean = 4.44). Those respondents from states most advanced in implementing reform tended to agree (mean = 3.22) as compared to the less advanced groups (mean range from 4.1 through 4.8). The observed differences, however, are not statistically significant ($F = 1.7$, $p > 0.05$).

Yet, in response to a statement more narrowly focused on program funding practitioners were less ambivalent. Table 19 presents respondents' levels of agreement with the claim that performance budget reform has little influence on political decision-makers' determinations of program funding. This table shows that the overall mean indicated agreement with this claim and that the level of agreement does not vary in a statistically significant way across

Table 17. Level of Agreement That Reporting of Performance Measures and Standards In Budgeting Increases Discretion Over the Timing or Allotment of Funds, Difference by Group.

Source	D.F.	Analysis of Variance Sum of Squares	Mean Squares	*F* Ratio	*F* Prob.
Between Groups	5	13.2867	2.6573	1.1905	0.3170
Within Groups	138	308.0396	2.2322		
			Mean[a]	Std Dev	N[b]
For Entire Population			4.8403	1.4990	144
GROUP 1 Very advanced			3.7778	0.8333	9
GROUP 2 More advanced			4.6111	1.8830	18
GROUP 3 Somewhat advanced			5.0000	1.3416	11
GROUP 4 Not too advanced			4.9444	1.5712	54
GROUP 5 Preliminary stage			5.0270	1.3640	37
GROUP 6 No reform			4.8000	1.3732	15

[a] Scale for response: Strongly agree = 1, More than agree = 2, Agree = 3, Neutral = 4, Disagree = 5, More than disagree = 6, Strongly disagree = 7.
[b] Number of responses indicating performance measures not used (37). Number of missing observations (6).

different stages of implementing budget reform ($F = 1.67$, $p > 0.05$) or between respondents from budget offices or agencies ($F = 2.56$, $p > 0.05$). In spite of the lack of statistical significance, the data in Table 19 do illustrate two substantive trends. First, the degree of agreement that the use of performance measures does not impact funding decisions is lower among respondents from states most advanced in implementing reform. Second, the level of agreement is higher among agency administrators versus central budget analysts.

One reason why practitioners may hold definitive opinions on the question of funding decisions but be less certain about the broader issue of oversight focus is a respondent's view of the time required for such a general change to come about. Respondents from both agencies and central budget offices commented that a shift in politicians' oversight focus "would be slow" or "would probably take a long time". Many practitioners qualified their response by noting that their agreement or disagreement to this question was conditional, and that it depends on what happens in the future. This opinion was expressed, not only by respondents in states that had recently undertaken reform, but also by practitioners in states that had been advancing performance budget reform

Table 18. Level of Agreement That Reporting Performance Measures and Standards Changes Oversight Focus of Political Decisions Makers From Inputs Toward Results, Difference By Group.

Source	D.F.	Analysis of Variance Sum of Squares	Mean Squares	*F* Ratio	*F* Prob.
Between Groups	5	19.7427	3.9485	1.7038	0.1377
Within Groups	138	319.8128	2.3175		
			Mean[a]	Std Dev	N[b]
For Entire Population			4.4444	1.5409	144
GROUP 1 Very advanced			3.2222	1.5635	9
GROUP 2 More advanced			4.1111	1.2783	18
GROUP 3 Somewhat advanced			4.5364	1.8040	11
GROUP 4 Not too advanced			4.4630	1.5867	54
GROUP 5 Preliminary stage			4.6757	1.4153	37
GROUP 6 No reform			4.8000	1.5675	15

[a] Scale for response: Strongly agree = 1, More than agree = 2, Agree = 3, Neutral = 4, Disagree = 5, More than disagree = 6, Strongly disagree = 7.
[b] Number of responses indicating performance measures not used (37). Number of missing observations (6).

for many years. Certainly, this statement provoked the greatest number of comments on the questionnaire. It also produced the most equivocal answers. As one practitioner put it": This [shift in focus] is the key variable, but who can predict what they [legislators] are going to do".

Greater Control

Overall, it was proposed that control of legislators and central budget staff over agencies in the budget process would not be perceived to be devolved but rather strengthened with the implementation of performance budget reform. However, among the majority of respondents, greater control by legislators and central budget staff was not perceived to accompany the reporting of performance measures and standards in the budget process. Yet interestingly, practitioners from states most advanced in implementing budget reform agreed more often than those in less advanced states ($F = 2.29, p < 0.05$). As illustrated in Table 20, while other groups were in the neutral to disagree range (mean range 4.2 to 4.6), the means for respondents from Group 1 indicated agreement (mean = 3.0).

Table 19. Level of Agreement That Reporting Performance Measures Has Little Influence on Political Decision Makers In Determining Program Funding, Difference By Group and Organization.

		Analysis of Variance			
Source	D.F.	Sum of Squares	Mean Squares	*F* Ratio	*F* Prob.
Main Effects					
GROUP	5	23.272	4.654	1.678	0.144
ORG	1	7.109	7.109	2.562	0.112
2-way Interactions					
GROUP ORG	5	12.798	2.560	0.923	0.469
		Mean[a] Budget Office	Std Dev Budget Office	Mean Agency	Std Dev Agency
For Entire Population		3.3889	1.6746	2.9726	1.6913
GROUP 1 Very advanced		5.0000	1.4142	3.4000	0.1402
GROUP 2 More advanced		3.3000	1.7029	3.7500	2.1876
GROUP 3 Somewhat advanced		2.8571	1.5736	1.4000	0.8944
GROUP 4 Not too advanced		3.3333	1.5442	3.2500	1.9365
GROUP 5 Preliminary stage		3.4118	1.8391	2.5556	1.1991
GROUP 6 No reform		3.2857	1.9760	2.8889	1.3642

[a] Scale for response: Strongly agree = 1, More than agree = 2, Agree = 3, Neutral = 4, Disagree = 5, More than disagree = 6, Strongly disagree = 7.

This finding is consistent with the literature on reform that outlines its dual objectives of both giving "units greater operational autonomy while developing a greater steering and strategic control capability at the central level" (OECD, 1994, p. 54) or as Cothran (1993, p. 450) describes it, greater control over "priorities " and "evidence of program achievement" in exchange for increased discretion over how appropriated funds are spent.

Legal Accountability

Although an administrator's accountability to the law is outside the prescriptions of performance budget reform, discussions in the literature of accountability and budgeting indicate its importance. A third question raised in this research was:

3. Do legal accountability claims limit the amount of administrative discretion in budgeting that can be realized from the implementation of performance budget reform?

Table 20. Level of Agreement That Control of Legislators and Central Budget Staff Is Increased With The Implementation of Performance Budget Reform, Difference By Group.

		Analysis of Variance			
Source	D.F.	Sum of Squares	Mean Squares	*F* Ratio	*F* Prob.
Between Groups	5	21.3162	4.2632	2.2990	0.0483
Within Groups	138	255.9061	1.8544		
			Mean[a]	Std Dev	N[b]
For Entire Population			4.3611	1.3923	144
GROUP 1 Very advanced			3.0000	1.0000	9
GROUP 2 More advanced			4.5556	1.0966	18
GROUP 3 Somewhat advanced			4.5455	1.5725	11
GROUP 4 Not too advanced			4.5926	1.2815	54
GROUP 5 Preliminary stage			4.2703	1.4462	37
GROUP 6 No reform			4.2000	1.6987	15

[a] Scale for response: Strongly agree = 1, More than agree = 2, Agree = 3, Neutral = 4, Disagree = 5, More than disagree = 6, Strongly disagree = 7.
[b] Number of responses indicating performance measures not used (37). Number of missing observations (6).

While the importance of legal constraints is expected to vary across programs and states, for practitioners in all areas it was proposed that: (1) laws and the courts interpretation of them will be perceived as placing significant limits on administrative discretion in budgetary decision making and (2) administrative discretion in budgeting is perceived to be impacted significantly by mandates between levels of government and across branches of government.

Overall, 64% of respondents ($N = 185$) perceived change in the laws which restrict an administrator's discretion in budgetary decisions to be at least substantially important in realizing a performance based budgeting process and 38% of these respondents found it more than substantially important. Similarly, a majority of respondents felt strongly (agreed/strongly agreed) that legal constraints limited administrative discretion in responding to three of four statements regarding enabling statutes, funding decisions, and legal mandates.

Table 21 summarizes practitioners' responses to these four statements. Statement one claimed that a program's enabling statute significantly limited an administrator's discretion in making budget decisions. A sizeable number,

Table 21. Level of Agreement That Legal Constraints Limit Administrative Discretion In Budgetary Decisions.

Statement	More strongly agree 1 & 2 *N* %	Agree 3 *N* %	4 *N* %	Disagree 5 *N* %	More strongly disagree 6 & 7 *N* %	Median
One	38 20.5	59 31.9	32 17.3	40 21.6	16 8.7	3.0
Two	45 24.2	61 32.8	28 15.0	37 19.9	15 8.1	3.0
Three	40 21.5	57 30.6	35 18.8	44 23.7	10 5.4	3.0
Four	45 24.5	36 19.6	25 13.6	42 22.8	36 19.5	4.0

52.4%, had definite opinions (agreed/strongly agreed) that they did. The second item stated that constitutional provisions, federal mandates, and/or court degrees significantly limited an administrator's ability to make spending decisions based on his knowledge of program needs. Here too, a majority of respondents, 57%, agreed that legal mandates from other branches of government and between levels of government affected administrative discretion.

Statement three asserted more strongly that answerability to the law will dominate how annual budget decisions are made regardless of program results. Fewer than 30% of respondents rejected the statement while a total of 52% of practitioners agreed or strongly agreed. Finally, it was claimed that a significant portion of the current fiscal year's operating budget was determined by constitutional provisions, federal mandates, and/or court decrees. While 44% agreed with the statement, a comparable number (42%) disagreed or strongly disagreed that legal mandates significantly impacted their budget.

One respondent provided some useful insight into why survey participants may not perceive legal constraints as impacting their budgets. In his opinion, while there was no question that public administrators are held accountable to the law, "the law doesn't change that often, at least not relative to the annual cycle of the budget process". Instead he maintained that "the agency mission and the budget that carries it out reflect long standing legal mandates that don't affect the budget much from year to year".

Table 22. Percent of Operating Budget Determined By Constitutional, Federal and/or Court Mandates, Difference By Program Area.

		Analysis of Variance			
Source	D.F.	Sum of Squares	Mean Squares	*F* Ratio	*F* Prob.
Between Groups	2	7.2523	3.6262	40.6867	0.0000
Within Groups	128	11.4078	0.0891		

	Grp 1	Grp 2	Mean	Std Dev	N[a]
Grp 2 Revenue			0.1200	0.2061	37
Grp 1 Corrections		*	0.3130	0.3118	46
Grp 3 Education K-12	*	*	0.6889	0.3422	48

[a] Number of responses indicating percentage not known: Revenue (3); Corrections (3); Education K-12 (4). Number of missing observations: Revenue (14), Corrections (16); Education (16).
* Denotes pairs of groups significantly different at the 0.01 level.

Along with their opinions on budget impact, respondents were asked to assess the portion of their budget determined by legal mandates in percentage terms. As illustrated in Table 22 respondents in revenue areas, on average, reported that 12% of their operating budget was determined by legal mandates.

Table 23. Level of Agreement That Enabling Statutes Limit Administrative Discretion In Budgetary Decisions, Difference By Program Area.

		Analysis of Variance			
Source	D.F.	Sum of Squares	Mean Squares	*F* Ratio	*F* Prob.
Between Groups	2	38.7325	19.3662	9.9505	0.0001
Within Groups	182	354.2189	1.9463		

	Grp 3	Mean	Std Dev	N[a]
Grp 1 Corrections	*	3.9077	1.3661	65
Grp 2 Revenue	*	3.9444	1.3793	54
Grp 3 Education K-12		2.8990	1.4355	66

[a] Number of missing observations: Education K-12 (2).
* Denotes pairs of groups significantly different at the 0.01 level.

Table 24. Level of Agreement That Constitutional Provisions, Federal Mandates and/or the Courts Limit Administrative Discretion, Difference by Program Area.

Source	D.F.	Analysis of Variance Sum of Squares	Mean Squares	*F* Ratio	*F* Prob.
Between Groups	2	21.8006	10.9003	5.4449	0.0050
Within Groups	183	366.3553	2.0019		

	Group 1	Group 3	Mean	Std Dev	N[a]
Grp 1 Corrections			3.3718	1.4544	65
Grp 2 Revenue	*	*	3.9794	1.3312	54
Grp 3 Education K-12			3.0605	1.4410	67

[a] Number of missing observations: Education K-12 (1).
* Denotes pairs of groups significantly different at the 0.01 level.

This significantly varied from corrections and education, which reported 31% and 69% respectively ($F=40.6$, $p<0.01$).

Indeed, Tables 23 and 24 indicate that practitioners' opinions on legal accountability claims significantly varied according to program area. Overall, respondents in revenue reported the least impact, those in corrections perceived being more affected by enabling statutes ($F=9.95$, $p<0.01$), as well as court decrees, federal mandates, and constitutional provisions ($F=5.44$, $p<0.01$). Respondents in the area of education, however, perceived legal constraints as having the greatest effect on administrative discretion in budget decisions. These results are in keeping with the literature that argues, in certain program areas such as education, larger portions of budgets are "earmarked" for rights-based programs (Bunch & Straussman, 1993, Straussman, 1988).

Fiscal Constraints

A fourth research question is: Do fiscal constraints restrict the exercise of an administrator's own judgment in determining program spending?

While the extent of restriction imposed by fiscal constraints is expected to vary across programs and states, for practitioners in all areas it is proposed that: (1) fiscal constraints on budgets due to less money available and, (2) fiscal constraints on budgets due to less discretion in spending the funds that are available are perceived as significant limits to the exercise of an administrator's own judgment in program spending.

Overall, 68% of respondents ($N = 181$) perceived a lessening of fiscal constraints, both in terms of more dollars available and more dollars available that are not restricted to specific programs, to be at least substantially important in realizing a performance based budgeting process and 38% of these respondents found it more than substantially important. Similarly, a majority of respondents agreed or strongly agreed that fiscal constraints limited administrative discretion in budgeting decisions in responding to three of four statements concerning the dollars available, means of financing, compulsory adjustments, and automatic funding adjustments (e.g. indexing). Table 25 summarizes practitioners' responses to these four statements.

Statement one claimed that the means of financing (e.g. user fees, interagency transfers, statutory dedications) posed significant restrictions on the budget decisions administrators can make. A substantial number, (64%) of respondents agreed or strongly agreed with this statement. The next statement sought respondents' opinions on compulsory adjustments common to all state agencies (e.g. merit pay, group insurance) asserting that they significantly limit the flexibility administrators have in their program's budget decisions. Of the 186 responses, a total of 94 or 51% agreed.

Statement three proposed that multiyear, automatic funding decisions, such as formula funding and indexing for inflation, significantly restricted discretion in making budget decisions. Only 38% of the respondents agreed with this

Table 25. Level of Agreement That Fiscal Constraints Limit Administrative Discretion In Budgetary Decisions.

Statement	More strongly agree 1 & 2 *N* %	Agree 3 *N* %	4 *N* %	Disagree 5 *N* %	More strongly disagree 6 & 7 *N* %	Mean	Median
One	65	54	24	24	18		
	35.1	29.2	13.0	13.0	9.7	3.2	3.0
Two	48	46	34	40	18		
	25.8	24.7	18.3	21.5	9.7	3.6	3.0
Three	33	36	35	48	31		
	18.0	19.7	19.1	26.2	17.0	4.0	4.0
Four	67	51	22	31	16		
	35.6	27.3	11.8	16.6	8.5	3.2	3.0

statement. What is more, a larger number of respondents (43%) disagreed or strongly disagreed.

This finding seems to contradict contemporary literature in public budgeting, particularly current discussions at the federal level on inflation indexes and the sizeable effect these automatic increases have on entitlement programs and overall spending. However, comments by respondents suggest that, at the state level, fiscal constraints, specifically tax and expenditure limitations, were reasons why automatic increases were not perceived as such limiting factors in state budget decisions as one budget analyst wrote: "We haven't funded inflation in 8 years! Agencies ask but they don't get it".

Related to tax limitations, central budget office analysts also explained that there were concerns about projected structural imbalances in their state budget. Forecasted growth in spending while tax revenues were restricted, barred any type of automatic funding increase, such as inflation funding from being put into effect.

Among questionnaire items addressing fiscal constraints, this statement was the only one where a statistically significant difference was observed between program areas ($F=7.88$, $p<0.01$). Not surprisingly, 35 of the 69 respondents (51%) who agreed or strongly agreed that automatic funding decisions, including formula funding, restricted their discretion in making budget decisions were in Education K-12 program areas. As shown in Table 26, respondents from this area, on average agreed (mean = 3.45), differing from

Table 26. Level of Agreement That Multiyear, Automatic Funding Decisions Significantly Restrict Administrative Discretion in Budget Decisions, Differences by Program Area.

		Analysis of Variance			
Source	D.F.	Sum of Squares	Mean Squares	*F* Ratio	*F* Prob.
Between Groups	2	35.4376	17.7188	7.8836	0.0005
Within Groups	180	404.5624	2.2476		
		Grp 3	Mean	Std Dev	N[a]
Grp 1 Corrections		*	4.4688	1.5220	64
Grp 2 Revenue		*	4.1346	1.4955	52
Grp 3 Education K-12			3.4478	1.4800	67

[a] Number of missing observations: Corrections (1), Revenue (2), Education K-12 (1).
* Denotes pairs of groups significantly different at the 0.01 level.

respondents in both corrections and revenue, who were on average, neutral to the proposition (means 4.1 and 4.6 respectively).

Statement four claimed that the dollars available for budget requests significantly limited the ability of administrators to make spending decisions based on their own judgement and knowledge of program needs. In total 63% of respondents agreed, with approximately 36% giving the proposition a stronger endorsement (more strongly agree). There were no significant differences across program areas or between agency and budget office practitioners.

There were, however, statistically significant differences ($F = 11.04$, $p < 0.01$) between organizational perspectives regarding whether the means of financing and compulsory adjustments posed significant restrictions on the budget decisions administrators can make. As illustrated in Table 27, budget analysts were less in agreement with the first statement than agency respondents, and on average were neutral regarding the limitations imposed by mandatory adjustments required of all state agencies ($F = 11.04$, $p < 0.01$).

Table 27. Level of Agreement That Fiscal Constraints Pose Significant Restrictions on the Budget Decisions Administrators Can Make, Difference by Organization.

Source	D.F.	Analysis of Variance Sum of Squares	Mean Squares	*F* Ratio	*F* Prob.
		Means of Financing			
Between Groups	1	26.6429	26.6429	11.0421	0.0011
Within Groups	183	441.5517	2.4129		
			Mean	Std Dev	N[a]
Budget Office			3.5870	1.7298	92
Agency			2.8280	1.3563	93
		Compulsory Adjustments			
Between Groups	1	27.2780	27.2780	11.0421	0.0005
Within Groups	183	404.8511	2.2003		
			Mean	Std Dev	N[b]
Budget Office			4.0000	1.5619	92
Agency			3.2340	1.4022	94

[a] Number of missing observations: Agency (2).
[b] Number of missing observations: Agency (1).

Table 28. Percent of FY97 Operating Budget Perceived as Discretionary, Difference By Respondent Organization and Program Area.

		Analysis of Variance			
Source	D.F.	Sum of Squares	Mean Squares	*F* Ratio	*F* Prob.
Main Effects					
Respondent Organization	1	0.332	0.332	3.437	0.066
Program Area	2	0.409	0.204	2.115	0.124
2-way Interactions					
Organization Area	2	0.051	0.026	0.265	0.768
			Mean	Std Dev	N[a]
Area 1 Corrections			0.304	0.343	51
Area 2 Revenue			0.254	0.316	52
Area 3 Education K-12			0.178	0.274	52
Org 0 Budget Office			0.292	0.332	75
Org 1 Agency			0.196	0.289	73

[a] Number of responses indicating percentage not known: Corrections (2); Revenue (1); Education K-12 (3). Number of missing observations: Corrections (12), Revenue (7); Education K-12 (13).

Similar to the question on legal constraints, respondents were asked to assess the percentage of the agency's budget request in FY 97 that was discretionary, that is, not determined by multiyear, automatic funding decisions, mandates from other levels or branches of government, statewide adjustments, or ties to specific revenue sources. The average percentage reported does vary according to program area reflecting the pattern seen under legal constraints, however, not significantly so ($F=2.11$, $p>0.05$). Yet, what is notable is how much the addition of fiscal constraints is perceived to limit discretion in budgeting. Table 28 shows that respondents in all program areas from both budget offices and agencies perceived a low percentage of one-third or less of their FY 97 operating budget as discretionary.

Administrative Discretion

While each of the previous questions addresses particular accountability claims and constraints identified in the literature, the overarching research question of this is: Does performance budget reform increase the discretion of administrators in budget decisions better enabling them to use their expertise and knowledge of program needs to achieve program goals?

Based upon the theoretical rationales drawn from the literature, it was proposed that practitioners would not perceive that the implementation of performance budget reform increased administrative discretion in the manner prescriptive theory envisions no matter how far advanced in implementing reform. Also, legal and fiscal constraints, outside the scope of reform, were expected to affect administrative discretion in budget decisions, and therefore, the change performance budget reform could realize.

Table 29 shows that, in the aggregate, 64% of respondents perceive legal accountability claims to be at least substantially important in realizing a performance oriented budget process. As previously discussed, in response to specific questions regarding enabling statutes, constitutional provisions and mandates between levels and across branches of government, it was found that a majority of respondents agreed that legal constraints limited administrative discretion in budget decisions. Yet, consistent with the literature, the degree to which an agency's operating budget was perceived to be affected by legal constraints significantly varied according to program area.

Overall, this table illustrates that 68% of respondents think that fiscal constraints are important factors in realizing a performance based budget process. As noted earlier, practitioners, on average agreed that the means of financing and to a lesser extent, compulsory adjustments restricted administrative discretion in budgeting. However, the level of agreement varied according to the organizational perspective of respondent. Furthermore, automatic funding decisions, such as indexing for inflation were not found to be restrictive by a majority of respondents. Even so, the percentage of an agency's operating budget that was viewed as discretionary by respondents was estimated to be less than one third for all program areas by both agency administrators and central budget staff.

As noted in Table 29, 29% of respondents thought that reducing bureaucratic rules, procedures, and reporting requirements was substantially important and 35% thought they were more than substantially important in promoting the ability of administrators to utilize their professional expertise in budgetary decisions. Yet, in contrast to the predictions of reformers, perceptions among respondents regarding a streamlining of bureaucratic constraints were not found to vary according to the stage of reform. Respondents in all groups, perceived on average, that budget guidelines increased, performance measurement information did not substitute for traditional reporting requirements, and overall, more resources were expended in the administration of the annual/biennial budget process. These opinions did not significantly change when controlled for organization size, program area, or respondent's position.

Table 29. Perceived Importance of Change in Accountability Claims In Realizing A Performance Oriented Budget Process.

Accountability claim	Critically important 1 N (%)	2 N (%)	Substantially important 3 N (%)	4 N (%)	Slightly important 5 N (%)	6 N (%)	Not important 7 N (%)	Total Respondents
Bureaucratic: Reduction of administrative rules, procedures, guidelines and reporting requirements in the budget process	27 14.8	36 19.8	52 28.6	31 17.0	25 13.7	6 3.3	4 2.7	182
Political: Shift in political decision makers oversight focus from dollar inputs to program results	58 32.0	55 30.4	38 21.0	14 7.7	12 6.6	1 0.6	3 1.7	181
Legal: Change in the laws which restrict an administrator = s ability to use his own discretion in budgetary decision making	28 15.5	41 22.7	46 25.4	31 17.1	24 13.3	6 3.3	6 2.8	181
Fiscal: A lessening of fiscal constraints, both in terms of more dollars available and more dollars available that are not restricted or tied to specific programs	31 17.1	38 21.0	54 29.8	23 12.7	23 9.9	18 5.0	9 4.4	181

From the standpoint of statistical significance, there were no significant differences observed between groups that were more developed in implementing reform in terms of a devolution of political control in the transfer or allotment of funds. However, as outlined previously, respondents from the states most advanced in implementing performance budget reform did attribute greater flexibility in funding format and less itemization in appropriations to the use of performance measures and standards in the budget process. Though few in number, these practitioners did hold substantively important different opinions from other respondents and perceived a positive relationship between performance budget reform and increased administrative discretion with respect to a devolution of political control in the form of appropriations.

In keeping with the traditional criticisms of budget process reform in the literature, change in political accountability claims are considered most important in realizing a performance based budgeting process. As shown in Table 29, 85% of respondents view this change as at least substantially important in bringing about reform and nearly one-third perceive it as critically important. Moreover, the use of performance measurement information by political decision makers was a basic theme of comments made by survey participants.

Practitioners' Comments On Performance Budget Reform

Respondents were asked if there were factors other than the accountability claims outlined on the questionnaire that they thought were important in realizing a performance oriented budget process – one that would promote the ability of administrators to utilize their professional expertise and knowledge of program needs in budget decisions. Some spoke in broader terms of factors similar to those addressed in the survey instrument, such as the need for the legislature to stop "micro-managing and allow administrators to administer" or for "restrictions on how we do things to be substantially reduced".

Among the different suggestions offered were: a lessening of legislative budget staff power, greater clarity and agreement by political decision makers (legislators/governor) on the outcomes they want, more training and dollars invested to get the performance data that are really needed, two year budget cycles that free administrators and staff time for research, planning and management, and incentive based funding, the ability to fund projects using surplus dollars. Yet, the factor most frequently mentioned was the use of performance measurement information in budget decision making.

Both in written comments and telephone discussions many respondents indicated that they did not necessarily view the current budget reform initiative as "new".[2] Some perceived today's emphasis on outcomes or budget results as a continuing development of performance measurement information begun under program budgeting reforms of the 1970s and 1980s. Others view today's reform not as part of an ongoing process, but as a renewed attempt to incorporate performance measures in budgeting that was "unsuccessful before" or that "had been dormant for a number of years".

However, what was perceived as different by practitioners, who had been through a number of earlier attempts at budget reform, was the fact that state legislatures were codifying into law performance-based changes in budgeting. If the legislature had a stake in performance based reform initiatives it was believed politicians might be more inclined to use it or at least administrators "would have a highly visible policy statement to point to".[3] Another reason practitioners were more optimistic that today's initiative would bring about change was technology. Performance measurement information is now easier to access and therefore easier to use in making budget decisions.

These comments suggest that, as in the past, answerability to political decision makers is viewed as a formidable and largely an uncertain factor in realizing hoped for changes from reform. Legal and bureaucratic accountability demands, along with fiscal constraints, were proposed and also perceived by practitioners as limits on the discretion administrators have in making budget decisions. While the study did not detect many significant differences across respondents from states at varying stages of reform, it did show a divergence between the expectations established by reforms proponents and the viewpoints of practitioners on the changes that reform has brought about.

NOTES

1. Following are reasons why thirty-two practitioners would not or could not participate in the survey. Two state agency administrators and one budget analyst who had planned to respond did not due to illness. Four state agency administrators declined to participate. Three budget analysts declined because their office had a policy not to participate in opinion surveys. One top agency administrative post was vacant and three were newly appointed (less than a month) and did not feel qualified to respond. Six budget analysts also telephoned to say that they were recently hired and didn't feel they knew enough yet to answer the questions. Five agency administrators and seven budget analysts returned follow-up calls to say that they were just too busy with the upcoming year's budget to fill out a questionnaire. One explained that he usually attempts to respond to all surveys but due to present budget constraints in his state, this fall's negotiations between the agencies and the budget office were taking much more time.

2. Respondents provided written comments on the questionnaire and included memos and letters that expanded on closed ended responses of the survey instrument. Also, during both phases of primary data collection (i.e. the status of performance budget reform and opinions of administrative discretion) forty-eight telephone

discussions were conducted with respondents on substantive issues regarding clarification of their position on the use of performance based budgeting in their state and interpretation of responses to questionnaire items.

3. A similar opinion has been expressed at the federal level by the U.S. General Accounting Office (GAO) in a comparison of the Government Performance Results Act (GPRA) to federal reform efforts since 1950. The GAO claims that the "statutory foundation" of today's reform differentiates it from earlier initiatives and "should enhance [its] long-term prospects" (Curro, 1996, p. 6).

VI. A PERSPECTIVE ON PERFORMANCE BUDGET REFORM

In Chapter V, the results of the statistical analyses of the survey data were presented. This chapter discusses and interprets these results from the broader perspectives of both theory and practice. First, the interpretation of these results are presented with respected to changes in bureaucratic and political accountability claims that are expected from performance budget reform. Second, the results of the data analyses regarding legal accountability claims and fiscal constraints, which are largely outside the scope of performance budget reform, but which affect discretion in budget decision making, are discussed. Next, the implications of the results for public administrators attempting to implement performance budgeting and will be examined. Finally, suggestions for further related research will be presented.

INTERPRETATION OF RESULTS

Bureaucratic Accountability

A major premise of today's reform initiatives is that government bureaucracies should be freed from many of the constraints on how they operate. Performance budget reform proposes to reorient budgeting from compliance with rules to a focus on performance by freeing administrators from ex ante controls while holding administrators more accountable for the program results that budgets finance. However, in the opinion of respondents in the three program areas surveyed, reform has not yet made a major contribution toward such a change.

In contrast to the prediction of advocates, respondents did not perceive that bureaucratic constraints were streamlined with the implementation of this budget reform. To the contrary, performance budget reform was perceived to add to, not replace or lessen the number of rules, regulations and reporting requirements administrators must comply with in the administration of the budget process. There were no significant differences observed across respondents at different stages in implementing reform, nor did opinions vary by program, program size or respondent's position as an agency administrator or central budget office analyst.

Such broad consensus among respondents across all states makes visible a notable difference between the perceptions of practitioners and objectives of this reform as outlined by advocates. This finding, however, corresponds to assessments of past initiatives that described increases in the rules, regulations, paperwork and administrative burdens accompanying the adoption of various budget reforms (e.g. Howard, 1973; Lauth, 1979; Rose, 1977; Schick, 1973; Wildavsky, 1992b). It furthermore is consistent with recent reviews of performance budget initiatives at the federal and state level that suggest performance measurement data may be added to, not replace, traditional reporting requirements in the budget process (Berry, Brower & Flowers, 2000; Carroll, 1995; Curro, 1995, 1996; GAO, 1993, 1994; Jones, 1993; Joyce, 1993a, Jones & McCaffery, 1993).

Yet with some optimism, the data suggest that the additional time, people, and money required in administration of the annual/biennial budget process accompanying the adoption of this reform are not viewed as excessive by practitioners. Indeed, all respondents, on average, agreed that the reporting of performance measures and standards increased the resources expended in budget administration. Even so, they all also, on average, were either neutral or disagreed that this was "too much".

These results, however, could be due to the respondents surveyed. Top administrators and central budget staff were appropriate for this study because they are familiar with, not only budget decision making within a particular agency, but also the state's budget process. Yet to these people, performance measurement data may provide new information about programs. Practitioners at lower levels, who manage the programs and who may already know this information, may find the reporting of performance measures in budgeting duplicative or excessive and hold less positive views.

Another interpretation is that the extra administrative effort required under performance budgeting may not be perceived as excessive because technology makes such information less burdensome to generate and manage. Five states reported that they have already established centralized management information systems to integrate budgeting, accounting and performance data and sixteen more states report such a system is under development. Increasing sophistication in computer applications in budgeting and in reporting financial and nonfinancial measures is likely to continue. As Lee and Burns (2000) point out, "governments are unlikely to return to earlier systems that produced less

Table 30. Budget Formats in the States.

State Budget Processes	All States 1987	All States 1992	All States 1996
Budget format of agency requests			
Line item	1	10	2
Line item & program	8	4	4
Line item & org. unit	0	0	2
Line item, org. unit & program	23	13	17
Line item, organizational unit, program & lump sum	17	18	22
Program	0	2	1
Other	0	3	2
No report	1	0	0
Budget format of executive budget submitted to legislature			
Line item	8	9	5
Line item & org. unit	3	1	1
Line item & program	4	4	4
Line item, org. unit & program	14	7	11
Line item, organizational unit, program & lump sum	11	19	18
Organizational unit	1	1	3
Program	1	0	0
Other	4	7	8
No report	4	2	0
Budget format of appropriation bill			
Line item	13	11	15
Line item & org. unit	8	1	5
Line item & program	8	4	3
Line item, org. unit & program	2	3	5
Line item, org. unit, program & lump sum	7	15	14
Organizational unit	1	5	2
Program	0	1	0
Lump sum	1	4	1
Other	6	2	5
No report	4	4	0

Source: NASBO (1987); NASBO (1992); Survey data for this study (1996).

information" (p. 52). In the future this may mean that increased system support for implementing performance budgeting could, if not reduce the number of bureaucratic rules, procedures and reporting requirements, lessen the administrative burden of compliance.

Political Accountability Claims

Contrary to reform's expectations, it was proposed that with the advancement of reform political decision makers would not grant administrators greater discretion in fund management nor would legislative oversight be perceived to have shifted from dollar inputs toward the broader view, results achieved. Instead, the adoption of performance budget reform would be perceived to strengthen control of central budget staff and legislators over administrators in the budget process.

In the budgeting literature, state policy makers and central budget staff are reported to have strengthened their control over spending priorities and dollar ceilings (Lee, 1992; LeLoup, 1988; Schick, 1990). The results of past reform efforts also lend support to the position that politicians cannot be assumed to be "a malleable substance" that will change when faced with more "rational" budget processes (Wildalsky, 1992b, p. 431). Moreover, it has been argued that why elected officials would now change their behavior from focusing on micro-level inputs to emphasizing results obtained from public programs has yet to be convincingly argued by proponents (Cox, 1994; Joyce, 1993b; Khademian, 1995).

Results of data analysis indicated that the majority of respondents did not perceive that, with the implementation of performance budget reform, political decision makers granted administrators increased discretion in fund management. This finding is consistent with other recent findings that indicate performance measures have little impact on legislative oversight or legislative funding decisions (e.g. Bloom & McGuire, 1995; Berry, Browner, & Flowers, 2000; Franklin, 1999; Jordan & Hackbart, 1999; Willoughby & Melkers, 2000). It is also supported by the budget formats used in the states.

As illustrated in Table 28, over ninety percent of all states continue to use line item budgeting along with other budget formats in agency budget requests. Over seventy-five percent of the states use multiple formats that include line items in the executive budget submitted to the legislature with little change in these percentages from nine or four years earlier. Similarly in 1996, eighty-four percent of all states use a line item format plus other budget formats in the appropriation bill. Moreover, the number of states requiring line item budget formats in the appropriation bill has gone up from prior years.

Likewise, there has been little change over time in the number of states whose agency officials are authorized to transfer appropriations. Table 31 shows that some change has occurred in transfer authority between appropriations within the same agency/department and across objects of expenditures within a program. Still, in forty-seven of the fifty states, agency officials may

Table 31. Transfer Authority and Allotment of Funds in States' Budget Processes.

State Budget Processes	All States 1987	All States 1992	All States 1996
Agency officials authorized to transfer (non-emergency) appropriations between:			
Programs in separate departments/agencies			
Yes	0	1	1
Yes, with certain restrictions	0	0	2
No	50	49	47
Programs within the same department/agency			
Yes	3	5	6
Yes, with certain restrictions	0	2	4
No	46	43	40
No report	1	0	0
Object classes within a program or budget unit			
Yes	9	18	19
Yes, with certain restrictions 1	5	3	
No	39	27	28
No report	1	0	0
Allotments apply to			
All agencies	nr	nr	8
All funds	nr	nr	1
All agencies & all funds	nr	nr	32
Select funds	nr	nr	1
Not apply	nr	nr	8

Source: NASBO (1987); NASBO (1992); Survey data for this study (1996).

not transfer funds across programs in different departments or agencies. Although prior year data is not available regarding allotments, forty-one of the fifty states reported in 1996 that allotments applied to all agencies and/or all funds.

This small change did correspond with results from the survey of practitioners. Respondents from the states most advanced in implementing reform did perceive some change in terms of the legislature using more flexible funding formats and less detailed instructions in appropriations giving administrators more discretion in fund management during budget execution. With respect to relaxation of control over agency transfers of funds and more administrative discretion over the allotment of funds, similar patterns of response were observed. Respondents from the states at the most advanced stage of reform tended to agree, whereas respondents from states at lesser stages of reform were neutral or disagreed.

From the standpoint of statistical significance, the study indicates that only at the highest level in implementing reform do any of the expectations of change in political accountability claims correspond to practitioners perceptions. While proponents may take hope in the findings, it is well known that the error relative to subjective survey response data is high. Thus, to reach conclusions through statistical analysis requires a degree of rigor and response stability which is difficult at best, and particularly suspect with the total number of cases in the most advanced group we are dealing with here. Though substantively interesting, given inescapable data limitations of so few states at this level of reform, the implication of this result is, therefore, best left to further examination of practitioners perceptions across other program areas as well as over time.

The data analysis does, however, underscore the continued importance of political accountability in realizing the changes expected from budget process reforms. Although respondents were neutral regarding the claim that performance budgeting shifts political decisions makers' oversight focus toward results, they noted in telephone interviews and in written comments on the survey that this was a critical factor. The explanation given for their ambivalence was the time required for such a change to take place. Practitioners in states that had recently adopted reform and in states that had been advancing performance budget reform for many years indicated that change in political decision-makers' focus, if it did occur, would be slow to come about. These findings are consistent with the more modest expectations suggested by prior reforms and opinions of scholars (e.g. Bloom & McGuire, 1995; Franklin, 1999; Halachmi, 1996; Lee, 1997; Mosso, 1999; Rubin, 1990;

White, 1994) who like Joyce (1996a) caution "would-be reformers not to expect too much too fast" (p. 75).

Legal Accountability Claims

Although an administrator's accountability to the law is outside the prescriptions of performance budget reform, the literature of accountability and budgeting indicate its importance (e.g. Frederickson, 1992; Lowi, 1993; Moe, 1994; Moe & Gilmour, 1995). The legal requirements by which public administrators must abide when they make their policies and implement their programs should be considered when evaluating a reform that promises to reduce red tape and empower program managers (Moon, 1999; Peters & Savoie, 1996).

Results of this study provide support for the hypothesis that legal accountability claims affect the amount of administrative discretion in budgeting that can be realized from the implementation of performance budget reform. Laws and the courts interpretation of them, as well as mandates between levels of government and across branches of government were perceived as placing significant limits on administrative discretion in budgetary decision making by a majority of respondents.

The study's results, furthermore, reinforce Straussman's (1986, 1988) argument that there is a need to differentiate among programs that have distinct claims on appropriations. These appropriations are unlike regular spending because they are protected by a moral or legal right to funding. The need to recognize separate categories of expenditures and their affect on discretion and choice in the budget process was demonstrated in the study by the different proportions of their budgets respondents perceived were determined by enabling statutes, court decrees, federal mandates, and constitutional provisions. The relatively low percentage (12%) of the operating budget reported by respondents in Revenue as restricted by legal constraints significantly varied from percentages reported in Corrections (31%) and Education K-12 (69%).

This finding suggest that statewide approaches to performance budget reform may benefit by evaluating the potential for change within defined program areas. Differentiating across program areas according to the discretion administrators have in their budget decisions would better align the expectation of change to come from performance budgeting with administrators ability affect such a change. More reasonable assessment of change may lessen frustration among budget actors and avoid further disillusionment by the public that comes from promises of budget reform that exaggerated the improvements that can be made.

Fiscal Constraints

Prescriptions for reform also do not directly address fiscal constraints, however, this study argues that it is important to acknowledge that the increase in performance measurement data in budgeting has taken and is taking place in the context of dollar limits. Pressures on public spending in the states have been related to less federal money available, economic conditions, and the public's resistance to higher taxes. Increased administrative discretion is regarded as a way of generating budget savings by allowing more innovative and entrepreneurial decisions and it often is considered a trade-off to cushion the effect of cuts (Jones, 1994; Cothran, 1993; Gray & Jenkins, 1993).

Overall, sixty-three percent of respondents agreed with the proposition that the dollars available for budget requests significantly limited the ability to making spending decisions based on an administrator's own judgement and knowledge of program needs. As expected, there were no significant differences across program areas or between agency and budget office practitioners. This finding supports the contention of Jones (1994) and others (e.g. Dupont-Morales & Harris, 1994; Sorensen 1994; Rubin, 1995; Wilson & Sylvia, 1993) that fiscal constraints narrow the choices available to public managers and reenforce an emphasis on top-down spending controls.

Similarly, a majority of respondents agreed with the position in the literature (e.g. Bunch & Straussman, 1993; Hackbart & Carlson, 1993) that fiscal constraints on budgets due to less flexibility in spending the funds that are available, limit administrative discretion in budgeting decisions. Both the means of financing and compulsory adjustments common to all state agencies were perceived by survey respondents as significantly restricting the flexibility administrators have in their program's budget decisions. However, multiyear, automatic funding decisions, such as formula funding and indexing for inflation, contrary to its emphasis in the budgeting literature was not perceived by most practitioners as restrictive with the exception of those respondents in the area of Education K-12.

Although this finding is only suggestive, it indicates an interesting difference between the issues affecting federal versus state budgeting. While indexing of entitlements is considered a large factor in the level of federal spending, in state budgets, which have balanced budget requirements, comments by practitioners suggest these constraints may not be restrictive because they are largely ignored under tight spending limits.

Also, respondents comments indicate that downward pressures on state spending can be due to an anticipated structural imbalance in a state's budget. This suggests that in budgeting research, the forecasted growth in future expenditures and revenues should be considered along with more standard measures for evaluating fiscal conditions in a state (e.g. current revenues, debt, expenditures, and per capita income of residents).

The data analysis related to fiscal constraints, furthermore, reemphasizes the need to differentiate among program areas in order to assess the changes that can be expected from this budget reform. Just as with legal constraints, the percentage of a program's budget perceived to be discretionary varied significantly by program area. Moreover, an important implication for proponents of performance budgeting is how low these percentages are perceived to be. Respondents in all program areas, on average, perceived no higher than thirty percent of their current operating budget was discretionary.

IMPLICATIONS

As outlined in Chapter I, an overall objective of this study was to bring practitioners' perceptions on the implementation of reform into a discussion that has largely been normative. As Rubin (1990) points out, to improve the relationship between budget theory and practice: "First, a better understanding is needed of what the budget process and format can and cannot do so that reform proposals are realistic" (p. 184). This study represents an initial attempt to explore one prescription of performance budget reform, increased administrative discretion. It relates the changes expected by reform's advocates to practice by soliciting practitioners perceptions on the implementation of performance budget reform in their state and its relationship to discretion and accountability in budget decision making.

Examining prescriptions of performance budget reform in terms of the experience gained from using them in practice fills a gap in the literature; however, it is important to note the limitations of using empirical data that are primarily self-reported. The study collected and analyzed data that were perceptual in nature and the accuracy of respondents' perceptions cannot be judged. However, the preliminary assessment of budget processes and performance budget reforms in the states strengthened the analysis of the data. Empirical data were also improved by seeking opinions from two different organizational viewpoints: agency administrators and central budget office staff. While recognizing these limitations, this study has important implications for budget practice.

Budget Practice

The implications for practice are significant particularly as states continue to adopt performance based systems in order to improve public budgeting. Although this trend in state budgeting has often been discussed, this study gathered data from each of the states to assess the changes that have been made. What is obvious from this phase of the research is that there has been great expansion in the development of more explicit standards and measures of performance in budgeting across the nation. Consistent with other recent findings on states' budgeting processes (e.g. Jordan & Hackbart, 1999; Lee, 1997; Lee & Burns, 2000; Willoughby & Melkers, 1999), states were found to vary in the scope and characteristic of performance budget reform. However, a large majority, forty of the fifty states, report an ongoing, centrally directed initiative to incorporate performance measures and standards, including outcome measures, into their budget process.

In analyzing practitioners' perspectives about these changes across the states in three program areas, the overall findings suggest that they do not perceive administration discretion in budget decision makingincreases with the advancement of reform. However, practitioners do indicate that they are answerable to multiple accountability claims and that these constraints limit their discretion in making budget decisions. For practice, this suggests that performance budget reform may be a more restricted process and be more difficult to accomplish than advocates recognize.

If as found here, a large percentage of a program's budget is determined by fiscal and legal claims, expectations of change that are to come from performance budgeting need to be lowered to reflect the actual influence that administrators have. A related implication is that expectations of reform may be more meaningful if distinctions between program areas and related differences in administrative discretion is considered. Not all categories of spending are equal (Straussman, 1988) and not all types of programs have the same potential for improvement from performance budgeting. Undertaking reform in a way that takes into account these differences may be more productive than implementing a uniform initiative statewide.

In a critique on the use of performance measures in federal budgeting, Joyce (1993b) made a similar observation noting that responsibilities vary widely from agency to agency and therefore, a deliberate approach is better than adopting a set of uniform requirements for all federal agencies. More recently, Radin (2000) has criticized the Government Performance and Results Act (GPRA)for emphasizing "commonalities rather than differences" and adopting a generic, "one size fits all approach" to reform (p. 113). Instead of a government-wide approach, Radin also thinks that "reform can best be handled in the context of specific program areas" that take into account "the constraints that are part of the American decision making process" (pp. 133–134).

Rules, procedures and reporting requirements were not perceived by respondents to be streamlined with the implementation of reform which suggests that bureaucratic constraints may be very hard to reduce. If so, lessening bureaucratic burdens may demand greater effort than has been expended to date. As noted in practitioners' comments, training and management information systems are perceived as necessary for improving implementation efforts. Giving people responsibility for results is not helpful if they are unable or unprepared to do it. Setting the context for change means understanding what administrators do and do not know and providing the training and support systems to help them succeed.

Today, when reform is also linked to cutbacks, this support is often not available. As shown in Table 32, training on performance measurement and monitoring has been provided to central executive budget staff and agency or program administrators in more than half of the states that have adopted reform. However, with few exceptions, the initiative is expected to be paid for from existing resources. Few states have appropriated additional funds for management information systems or to the agencies and central budget office for implementing performance budget reform. One implication is that, without funding, reformers need to carefully assess the feasibility and costs of performance-based budgeting. Certainly, this suggests governments must balance their ideal performance-based budgeting system against real-world considerations such as the dollars and effort involved in gathering, analyzing, and reporting performance data.

Finally, the study suggests state approaches to budget reform should be broadened. Attention needs to be focused on how reform can address other changes in accountability structures that shape existing constraints to administrative discretion (e.g. fund structures, intergovernmental mandates). Utilizing practitioners' expertise and experience in budgeting may be one way to begin. A common thread that runs through the opinions supplied by state practitioners in this study, is that the respondents – including state central budget staff who often represent the state's budget reform advocates – are knowledgeable and realistic about the challenges they confront.

FUTURE RESEARCH

Future research efforts should focus on extending the findings of this project and addressing some of the limitations of the study. One noted previously is the

Table 32. Implementation of State Reform Initiatives.

Types of System Support	Number of States With Budget Reform Initiative	Number of States Without Budget Reform Initiative*
Integration of budgeting, accounting & performance information systems		
Is available in a centralized management information system	5	0
Is under development as a centralized management information system	16	1
Is under development by individual agencies	2	0
Has not yet been addressed	17	3
Not apply	0	6
To facilitate the integration of performance measures in budget process, additional funds have been appropriated for management information systems		
Yes, in FY97	1	0
No, no appropriations in FY97	39	4
Not apply	0	6
Yes, in prior years	8	0
No, no appropriations in prior years	32	4
Not apply	0	6
Additional funds (excluding management info. systems) have been appropriated to central budget office		
Yes, in FY97	1	0
No, no appropriations in FY97	39	4
Not apply	0	6
Yes, in prior years	6	1
No, no appropriations in prior years	34	3
Not apply	0	6

Table 32. Continued.

Types of System Support	Number of States With Budget Reform Initiative	Number of States Without Budget Reform Initiative*
Additional funds (excluding management info. systems) have been appropriated to agencies/programs		
Yes, in FY97	1	0
No, no appropriations in FY97	39	4
Not apply	0	6
Yes, in prior years	1	1
No, no appropriations in prior years	39	3
Not apply	0	6
Training has been conducted for central executive budget staff on performance measurement & monitoring		
Yes, in FY97	23	1
No, no training provided in FY97	17	3
Not apply	0	6
Yes, in prior years	16	1
No, no training in prior years	24	3
Not apply	0	6
Training has been conducted for agency/program administrators on performance measurement & monitoring		
Yes, in FY97	27	2
No, no training provided in FY97	10	2
Not known	3	0
Not apply	0	6
Yes, in prior years	18	2
No, no training in prior years	19	2
Not known	3	0
Not apply	0	6

* State programs may report performance measures but on an ad hoc basis. States may centrally direct the reporting of performance measurement data but there is no on going initiatives to incorporate this information into the budget process.

focus on perspectives of top administrators and central budget officers. Although appropriate for this research, their responses may well differ from those of program managers and other practitioners at lower levels of the organization. Subsequent studies should examine the opinions of these different groups.

Another area mentioned earlier is the need to examine practitioners' perceptions across other program areas. While there were indications that some of the changes prescribed by performance budget reform were being realized in states that were the most advanced, too few cases were available to draw any conclusions. Examining additional program areas would also indicate whether other factors idiosyncratic to Corrections, Revenue and Education K-12 account for the findings reported here.

There is also a need for to examine change over time, as more states progress in their use of performance budgeting. One of the major limitations of this study is the use of cross-sectional analysis. Although cross-sectional analysis was appropriate to this study given the goal of examining the perceptions of practitioners whose states are at different stages in implementing reform, longitudinal studies linking perceptions in one period to later periods when performance budgeting has advanced should also be pursued.

In addition, it would be useful to examine performance budgeting in the states by looking at prior periods to better understand the discontinuities or adaptations from earlier reform initiatives. The review of states' budget processes and practitioners comments in this study indicate that knowledge of a state's history in budget reform aids in understanding administrators' viewpoints. As Lee and Burns (2000) point out institutional memory reminds current participants in the budget process of past failures and may bring about more realistic perceptions "about the effort required in revising budget systems" (p. 53).

The results of this research also suggest that performance budget reform, particularly with respect to change in political accountability demands, will require time, perhaps a long time. The findings reported here, therefore, should be viewed as preliminary. If in the future states are found to be effective in realizing change, further work needs to examine how long it takes and what, if any, other conditions are related to its success.

Certainly, more needs to be known about the costs associated with performance budget reform and if greater spending on implementation efforts affects change. This could be examined in terms of the effects of funding levels provided for personnel, training of personnel, and management information systems supporting performance-based budgeting. For example, few states reported that they audited performance data even though it is considered necessary for effective performance measurement systems. Is this because of the dollars available and, if so, what are the implications? Also, how are the resources expended on reform implementation viewed by the various actors (e.g. legislators, executive budget office staff, program administrators)? Are the benefits of performance-based budgeting perceived to outweigh the costs?

Further study on the perceptions of these actors regarding other expectations of performance budget reform is also needed. Research that pursues different types of questions such as: What are the incentives for program managers to report performance measures in the budget if: (1) administrative discretion is not believed to be enhanced and (2) performance measures aren't perceived to positively affect (i.e. increase) program funding? This type of inquiry builds upon the results found here and advances our understanding about the "existential situation" in which participants find themselves (Wildvasky, 1980, p. 78).

Past reform initiatives achieved limited success. If performance budget reform is to succeed, attention and effort must focus on the complexity of the endeavor. As argued here, there are multiple accountability demands and constraints – bureaucratic, political, legal and fiscal – which administrators must balance and which affect the ability to realize the goals of reform. It is possible that efforts to make the budget process more performance-based may not be possible until substantial changes have occurred in some or all of these areas.

VII. CONCLUSIONS AND A PROPOSAL

A broad purpose of this study has been to examine if the expectations of performance budget reform as prescribed in theory correspond with the impact of reform as perceived by practitioners. By examining practitioners' perceptions of changes that have been made in their budget process and comparing these observations to the predictions of reformers, it attempts to take a step forward in penetrating "the real world" of budgeting. This is an area Bunch and Straussman (1993, p. 19) maintain is under researched, particularly at the state level where the normative dimension of budget reform remains strong.

Furthermore, by exploring alternative accountability claims and how they affect assumptions on which performance budget reform is based, this study extends the traditional critique of budget reform, the politics of budgeting, to include bureaucratic and legal accountability claims as well as fiscal constraints. These added restrictions on administrative discretion in budget decision making integrate the contemporary literature streams of both budget theory and accountability providing an alternative framework for analyzing budget reform.

A central premise of this framework is the recognition that much of what occurs in budgeting can be traced to the need of public administrators to deal with situations that frequently involve diverse and external constraints. In making explicit the multiple accountability demands administrators are answerable to and which limit their actions, the difficulties practitioners face in realizing the desired changes from performance budgeting may be improved. Confronting the difficulties of changing the budget process is an important, though overlooked, contribution to the literature on budget reform that frequently focuses on proposals for change and on enumerating reasons why policy makers should adopt them.

This study also suggests that budget theory must better integrate multiple approaches to budget reform that extend beyond budget process initiatives aimed at finding technical and managerial solutions to budgeting problems. Such a single standard obscures the difficult task of responding to the plurality of interests involved in any change with some sense of balance and equal emphasis. Although focused on a specific prescription of reform, the study examined performance budgeting from a broadened perspective. Reconceptualizing budget reform in a way that better blends our knowledge of political, legal and fiscal change in budgeting acknowledges the complexity of today's budget process and the difficulties posed by democratic governance.

A PORTFOLIO APPROACH TO BUDGET REFORM

Approaching budget reform much like we approach financial investments may be a very useful way to rethink how we can improve budgeting. In order to increase returns and limit risk, financial advisors recommend a well designed portfolio. A portfolio is simply a collection of assets selected from a wide array of different investments. To construct an investment portfolio, a total program rather than single investments are considered. Since no one type of investment works best under all market conditions, an investor stands a better chance of finding profitable opportunities and avoiding major reverses if assets are diversified. In this way gains can be realized from a variety of investments, at the same time the losses are minimized by spreading risk across different types of assets (e.g. stocks, bonds, cash, etc.).

A portfolio strategy for investments is based upon the philosophy that a broad approach toward asset allocation should be adopted while putting all of one's eggs in a single basket should not (or else you may lose all of them when you fall). Applying this logic to budget reform, would counter the single, managerial approach toward improving budgeting that historically has characterized change initiatives in the states. Promises that PPBS, MBO, ZBB or performance-based budgeting would revolutionize how we spend the public's money would be as suspect as investing all of one's wealth in a stock that is billed as a sure thing, guaranteed to generate high returns. Such expectations are unrealistic in finance for they ignore the basic tenets of diversification and risk/return trade-offs and in public budgeting because they overlook the multiple accountability demands that characterize today's budget process.

As shown in Fig. 4, a portfolio approach to budget reform would recognize the alternative types of accountability claims reviewed in this study. While an investment portfolio is a collection of assets, a reform portfolio is made up of the different ways individuals and institutions are answerable, or held accountable, for spending the public's money. Unlike present and past reform initiatives, efforts would not be focused on management practices and

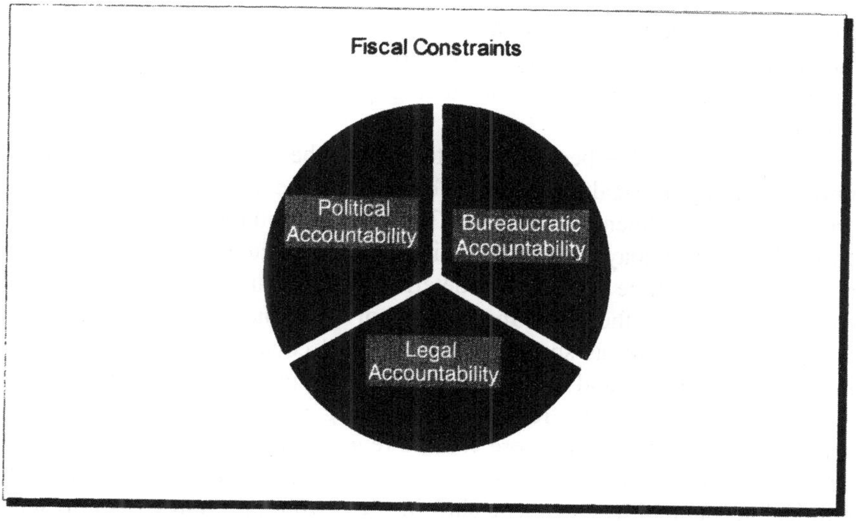

Fig. 4. A Portfolio Approach to Budget Reform.

bureaucratic change. To improve budgeting, reform in all accountability areas would be pursued. Such an approach would take advantage of multiple and diverse opportunities for change which may improve upon gains from "specific reforms such as Management by Objectives, PPB and ZBB [that] have been evaluated and declared to be failures" (Rubin, 1990, p. 180).

Furthermore, just as a portfolio is viewed as an integrated whole, so too are different accountability claims. The politics of budgeting is no longer perceived as a criticism of budget reform but, similar to its depiction in the current literature, an integral component of a complex, multi-faceted budgeting process. Change or improvement in budgeting would not be seen as thwarted by political accountability but would encompass it.

For example, change in political accountability may include requirements that legislative bodies make public the future costs of programs under consideration. That is, political decision making would take into account the time value of money and make these costs known to citizens/taxpayers prior to program authorization (Jones & Thompson, 1993; Thompson, 1994).

Reforming budgeting in terms of legal accountability could include making explicit, and if necessary, taking action to change, the percentage of funds that are restricted due to federal or local government mandates, earmarked revenues, and/or formula driven expenditures. These changes in budgeting, based on legal and political initiatives would be pursued along with changes in bureaucratic accountability, such as performance budget reforms. Moreover, all changes would be recognized as taking place with the context of fiscal constraints.

As was noted at the beginning of this book, the very concept of a budget implies scarcity or fiscal constraints. To again use the investment model, limits on resources do influence a portfolio. The amount required for investment in a particular vehicle may determine which one is selected. Along with dollars available, their source and stability determine the amount of loss that investors can absorbed and therefore the degree of risk and type of investments acceptable. Likewise, as shown in Fig. 5, fiscal constraints affect alternative accountability claims and the portfolio formulated to achieve budget reform.

In periods of declining revenues or shifting revenue streams from more stable (e.g. property tax) to more volatile (e.g. sales tax) dollars, budgets may be constrained and decision making more contentious. Hoped for changes in political accountability, such as a shift in focus from program costs to results, may be harder to achieve.

As illustrated, decline in revenues may result in cuts to programs with excellent performance. Reductions in personnel budgets may affect bureaucratic accountability and require that time and resources be expended on administrative tasks (e.g. the reporting of performance measures) rather than

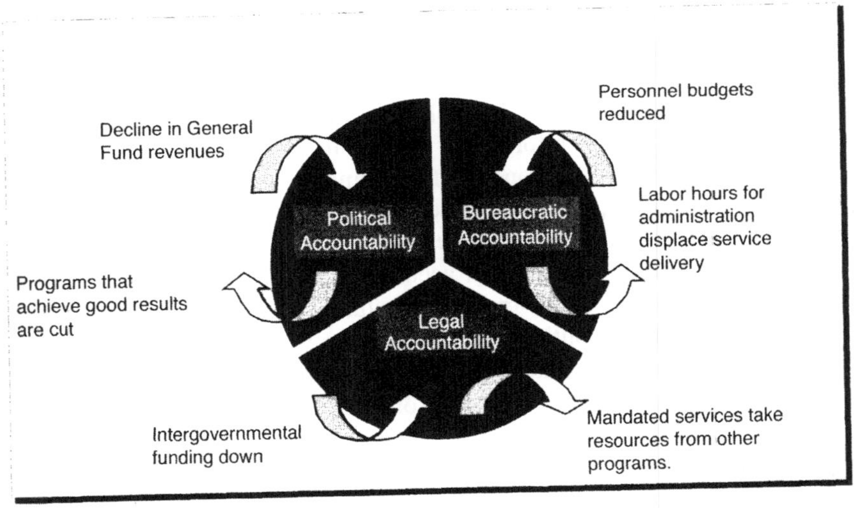

Fig. 5. Impact of Fiscal Constraints.

service delivery. Similarly, less intergovernmental funding for "rights based programs" such as health care for the medically needy and indigent may shift resources from other program areas and affect reform efforts.

While this study examined accountability claims in terms of performance budget reform's affect on administrative discretion, it should be pointed out that the limits to discretion identified often translate into increased fiscal constraints. For instance, agencies' compliance with more rules and reporting requirements, present under performance budget reform, not only limit discretion, but also increase resources expended on administration. Court rulings on due process and equal access can have sizable impact on discretion in decision making as well as discretionary dollars available to a government (e.g. education financing and entitlement programs) (Axelrod, 1989; Straussman, 1988). Elected officials refusals to increase taxes certainly affect how tight a budget may be. In sum, just as resources available influence investments and the investments chosen impact the gains realized, under a portfolio approach to budget reform, fiscal constraints both impact and are impacted by alternative accountability claims.

Using this model to frame our thinking about budget reform would also advance a much-needed contingency approach to change. The optimal structure for a portfolio is one that is best suited to the needs of the investor. There is no ideal mix of stocks, bonds or cash. Rather an appropriate asset allocation strategy reflects an individual's risk tolerance, time horizon and objectives. Constructing budget reforms in this way would make use of a mix of political, legal and bureaucratic change initiatives tailored to the level of government, actor, program, or other division under review.

A major concern of administrators regarding performance measures in budgeting, identified in this study and noted by others (e.g. Abney & Lauth, 1993; Broom & McGuire, 1995; Carroll, 1995; Franklin, Cawley & O'Sullivan-Katchel, 1998; Jones, 1993; Jordan & Hackbart, 1999; Joyce, 1993a; Willoughby & Melkers, 2000), is that legislators will not use them in appropriating funds or will use them only to make cuts. One reason is that the link between performance and resource allocation is not always straightforward. A program that has a good performance record will not necessarily be rewarded in the legislative budget process. Typically, there are many more well run programs than there are funds to finance them. Neither will a program that demonstrates poor performance always receive less funding. Funding levels may be mandated by law or the program may be underfunded to begin with and require more money to perform well. Because there is no clear, decision standard to apply, legislative budgetary decisions may not conform to the expectations of reformers.

Moreover, legislative budgetary decisions are seldom responsive to comprehensive analysis (Duncombe & Kinney, 1986; Elling, 1992). There is little political currency gained from attention to well run programs. Instead, attention is typically given to programs where problems are noted by constituents or interest groups. In other words, performance based budgeting may not be a reform well suited to elected officials because they have different objectives.

Similarly, the time horizon of elected officials may be limited to the period between elections. Achieving program outcomes based upon long term strategic goals is important. However, it may be less so to political actors due to their perceived need to realize results in two or four years. Under a portfolio approach, this would not indicate performance budgeting is an ineffective reform. However, it would mean that this reform is one better suited to budget actors, such as administrators, who have longer time horizons and whose objectives are primarily focused on program management.

The point has been made by others. Radin (2000) maintains that the types of data that are useful to multiple actors are quite different from one another. Moreover, he argues that "to believe . . . annual performance plans will answer the range of questions that emerge from these diverse actors is simply unrealistic" (p. 130). Many academics and practitioners find measures of efficiency, outputs and outcomes more appropriate for the technical/rational or managerial approach of decision making in the executive branch than to the political approach of decision making used by elected officials (e.g.Broom & McGuire, 1995; Brown & Pyers, 1998; Hendrick, 1996; Jones, 1993; Jordan & Hackbart, 1999; Joyce, 1993b; Radin, 2000; Roberts, 2000; Willoughby & Melkers, 2000).

Along with differentiating reform efforts by actors, under a portfolio approach the appropriate reform strategy would also be expected to vary across program areas. This study found that programs differ according to the proportion of their budgets determined by constitutional provisions, statutory formulae, and federal mandates. A portfolio framework would seek to tailor reform proposals to the particular constraints on budget decision making in a program area. That is, reformers would pursue changes in bureaucratic, political or legal accountability where the most gains could be made.

Also, reform initiatives would be adapted to the level of government. In the United States, federal, state and local budgeting processes are different (Bunch & Straussman, 1993; N. Caiden, 1994; Clynch & Lauth, 1991; Howard, 1973; Lynch, 1990 ; Rubin 1992; Wildavsky, 1986). Even so, as Schick (1988) points out, "since its emergence as a distinctive field a century ago, public administration has sought the 'one best way' to perform budgeting" (p. 60).

Today there are jurisdictions that are looked to as models for change (e.g. City of Sunnyvale, Fairfax County, State of Texas). Studies focus on select governments to discover what has or has not worked (CBO, 1993; GAO 1993, 1997). While further case study research is recommended because much can be learned from examining the success of a city or the experiences of states, the portfolio approach outlined here would emphasize the distinct features of each level of government along the accountability dimensions discussed.

It is feasible, for instance, that changing political decision makers' focus from program costs to results may be a simpler task at the local level such as a municipality with a city council or council-manager structure than at the state or federal level where larger numbers in the legislative body have to be convinced. Recognizing these differences, however, does not in any sense discount the value of knowing about others' experiences.

Information is valuable. In managing a portfolio of investments it is important to be as knowledgeable as one can, even about those investments that one cannot afford or that seem too risky. This knowledge provides a frame of reference for understanding one's own returns relative to others' and whether a different portfolio mix might be more profitable.

Information about other jurisdictions' experiences in budget reform or about the performance targets they achieve is valuable too. Not for the purpose of rendering judgement on one's own efforts or attempting to duplicating other governments' achievements, as Ammons (1999) puts it "that is not the point" (p. 108). Rather, information provides better understanding of past failures and indicates possible avenues of future success. However, success or failure, within a portfolio context, is a bounded notion. There is no single, fixed scheme that can be specified for all. To the contrary, the optimal structure of budget reform is one which reflects the particular objectives, challenges, and opportunities of the unit under review.

Reforming public budgeting requires a thoughtful allocation of effort across multiple accountability claims. Each is capable of advancing better budgeting, albeit in different ways. A portfolio framework provides a way to first recognized and then integrate fiscal constraints with bureaucratic, political and legal accountability claims. The findings of this study support the contention that these diverse and, at times, confounding constraints are features of public budgeting today.

Performance budget reform and its prescriptions for increased administrative discretion in exchange for accountability for results overlooks these alternative claims and in doing so, minimizes the difficulty in realizing reform. In the future, reforms must proceed from a base that is both better informed about and more understanding of the multiple accountability demands that are integral to change in budgeting.

The best chance for accomplishing this is by developing a theoretical rationale that advances a broadened, contingency approach to reform which highlights the value of pursuing diverse initiatives. Rethinking budget reform in this way would contribute to the development of descriptive theories that better explain the reality practitioners face in advancing reform. Theories that would not evade the difficult problems of designing change in our democratic system, but instead makes explicit these problems and provides a new basis for inquiry into their solution. Furthermore, approaching reform in this way may generate some novel, practical initiatives into which actual budget systems will fit.

If we've failed in the past to reform budgeting, then we need to profit from that failure and design initiatives that will make success as likely as possible. Unless we consider and improve upon all the accountability claims that affect budgeting, budget reform is likely to remain more hope than fact.

REFERENCES

Aberbach, J. D., & Rockman, B. A. (1988). Mandates or mandarins? Control and discretion in the modern administrative state. *Public Administration Review, 48*, 606–612.

Abney G., & Lauth, T. P. (1993). Determinants of state agency budget success. *Public Budgeting & Financial Management, 5*(1), 37–65.

Ammons, D. N. (1999). A proper mentality for benchmarking. *Public Administrative Review, 59*(2), 105–109.

Anders, K. (1996, October). *Accountability, Discretion, and Performance Budget Reform.* Paper presented at the Annual Conference of the Association for Public Budgeting and Financial Management, Washington, D. C.

Anthony, R. N. (1965). *Planning and control systems: A framework for analysis.* Boston: Harvard University.

Apostolou, N. G., Brooks, R. C., & Hildreth, W. B. (1992). Research and trends in government accounting and reporting. *International Journal of Public Administration, 15*(5), 1121–1149.

Appleby, P. (1957). The role of the budget division. *Public Administration Review, 17*, 156–158.

Arnold, P. (1995). Reform's changing role. *Public Administration Review, 55*, 407–417.

Axelrod, R. N. (1988). *Budgeting for modern government.* New York: St. Martin's Press.

Axelrod, R. N. (1989). *A budget quartet: Critical policy and management issues.* New York: St. Martin's Press.

Baldwin, J. W. (1990). Perceptions of public versus private sector personnel and informal red tape: Their impact on motivation. *American Review of Public Aministration, 20*, 7–28.

Barth, T. J. (1993). Constitutional subordinate autonomy: Serving multiple masters – a normative theory in practice. *Administration & Society, 25*(2), 160–182.

Bartle, J. R. (1999, April). *Yesterday, today and tomorrow: The evolution of budget theory.* Paper presented at the National Conference of the American Society for Public Administration, Orlando, Florida.

Barzelay, M. (1992). *Breaking through bureaucracy.* Berkeley: University of California Press.

Behn, R. D. (1985). Cutback budgeting. *Journal of Policy Analsis and Management, 4*, 155–177.

Behn, R. D. (1996, October). *The new public-management paradigm and the search for democratic accountability*. Paper presented at the annual research conference of the Association for Public Policy Analysis and Management, Pittsburgh, PA.

Berry, F. S., Brower, R. S., & Flowers, G. (2000). Implementing performance accountability in Florida: What changed, what mattered, and what resulted. *Public Productivity & Management Review, 23*(3), 338–358.

Berry, F. S., & Weschler, B. (1995). State agencies' experience with strategic planning: Findings from a national survey. *Public Administration Review, 55*, 159–168.

Bertram, G. M. (1978). The new systems budgeting. In: A. C. Hyde & J. M. Shafritz (Eds.), *Government budgeting: Theory, process, politics*. Oak Park, IL: Moore Publishiing.

Blalock, H. M. (1979). *Social statistics*. New York: McGraw-Hill.

Bledsoe, R. (1991). Coordination of budgeting. In: T. D. Lynch (Ed.), *Federal budget & financial management reform* (pp. 31–51). New York: Quorum Books.

Botner, S. B. (1985). The use of budgeting/management tools by state governments. *Public Administration Review, 45*, 616–620.

Bozeman, B. (1993). A theory of government "red tape". *Journal of Public Administration Research and Theory, 3*(3), 273–303.

Bozeman, B. & Loveless, S. (1987). Sector context and performance: A comparison of industrial and government research units. *Administration and Society, 19*, 197–235.

Bozeman, B., Reed, P., & Scott, P. (1992). Red tape and task delays in pubic and private organizations. *Administration and Society, 24*, 290–322.

Bozeman, B., & Straussman, J. D. (1982). Shrinking budgets and the shrinkage of budget theory. *Public Administration Review, 42*, 509–515.

Broom, C. A. (1996). *Performance-based government models: Continuing to build a track record*. Paper presented at the Annual Conference of the Association for Public Budgeting and Financial Management, Washington, D.C.

Broom, C. A., & McGuire, L. A. (1995). Performance-based government models: Building a track record. *Public Budgeting & Finance, 15*(4), 3–17.

Brown, R. E., & Pyers, J. B. (1998). Service efforts and accomplishments reporting: Has its time really come? *Public Budgeting & Finance, 18*(4), 101–113.

Brudney, J. L., Hebert, F. T., & Wright, D. S. (1999). Reinventing government in the American states: Measuring and explaining administrative reform. *Public Administration Review, 59*(1), 19–30.

Buchanan, B. (1975). Red-tape and the service ethic: Some unexpected differences between public and private managers. *Administration and Society, 6*, 423–444.

Bunch, B. S., & Straussman, J. D. (1993). State budgetary processes: The two faces of theory. *Public Budgeting & Financial Management, 5*(1), 9–36.

Bundt, J., & Lutz, G. M. 1999). Connecting state government reform with public priorities: The Iowa test case. *State and Local Government Review, 31*(2), 78–90.

Buschor, E., & Schedler, K. (Eds.). (1994). *Perspectives on performance measurement and public sector accounting*. Berne: Haupt.

Caiden, G. E. (1991). *Administrative reform comes of age*. New York: Walter de Gruyter.

Caiden, G. E. (1994). Administrative reform – American style. *Public Administration Review, 54*, 123–128.

Caiden, N. (1990). Public budgeting in the United States: The state of the discipline. In: N. Lynn & A. Wildavsky (Eds), *Public administration: The state of the discipline* (pp. 228–255). Chatham, NJ: Chatham House Publishers.

Caiden, N. (1994). Budgeting in historical and comparative perspective. *Public Budgeting & Finance, 14*(1), 44–57.

Campbell, M. D. (1994, October). Performance measures in government: A systemic view. *Conference Proceedings: Managing for results – Performance measures in government* (pp. 24–27). Austin, TX: University of Texas.

Carroll, J. (1995). The rhetoric of reform and political reality in the National Performance Review. *Public Administration Review, 55*, 302–312.

Chief Financial Officiers (CFO) Council, GPRA Implementation Committee. (1997, January). *Integrating performance measurement into the budget process*. [on-line] Available: http:// www.financenet.gov/gpra.htm.

Clynch, E. J., & Lauth, T. P. (Eds). (1991). *Governors, legislatures and budgets*. New York: Greenwood Press.

Coe, C. (1999). Local Government Benchmarking: Lessons from two major multigovernment efforts. *Public Administration Review, 59*(2), 110–123.

Cogan, J. F., Muris, T. J., & Schick, A. (Eds). *The budget puzzle: Understanding federal spending*. Stanford, CA: Stanford University Press.

Commission on Organization of the Executive Branch of Government. (1949). *Budgeting and Accounting*. Washington, D.C.: U.S. Government Printing Office.

Connelly, M., & Tompkins, G. L. (1989) Does performance matter? A study of state budgeting. *Policy Studies Review, 8*(2), 288–299.

Cothran, D. A. (1993). Entrepreneurial budgeting: An emerging reform? *Public Administration Review, 53*, 445–454.

Cox, R. W. (1994). The Winter Commission report: The practitioner's perspective. *Public Administration Review, 54*, 108–109.

Curro, M. (1995). Federal financial management and budgeting: NPR recommendations and GAO views. *Public Budgeting & Finance, 15*(1), 19–26.

Curro, M. (1996, October). *Connecting resources to results: A comparison of the Goverment Performance Results Act to federal efforts since 1950*. Paper presented at the Annual Conference of the Association for Public Budgeting and Financial Management, Washington, D. C.

DiIulio, J. J., Garvey, G., & Kettl, D. F. (1993). *Improving government performance: An owner's manual*. Washington, D.C.: The Brookings Institution.

Downs, G. W., & Larkey, P. D. (1986). *The search for government efficiency: From hubris to helplessness*. New York: Random House.

Drucker, P. (1954). *The Practice of Management*. New York: Harper & Row.

Drucker, P. (1964). *Managing for results*. New York: Harper & Row.

Dubnick, M. J. (1994). A coup against king bureaucracy. In: J. DiIulio (Ed.), *Deregulating the public service: Can government be improved?* (pp. 249–287). Washington, D.C.: The Brookings Institution.

Duncombe, S., & Kinney, R. (1986). Agency budget success: How it is defined by budget officials in five western states. *Public Budgeting & Finance, 7*(1), 24–37.

DuPont-Morales, M. A., & Harris, J. E. (1994). Strengthening accountability: Incorporating strategic planning and performance measurement into budgeting. *Public Productivity & Management Review, 17*(3), 231–239.

Durant, R. F. (1995). Public policy, overhead democracy, and the professional state revisited. *Administration & Society, 27*(2), 165–202.

Durant, R. F. (2000). Whither the neoadministrative state? Toward a polity-centered theory of administrative reform. *Journal of Public Administration Research and Theory, 10*(1), 79–109.

Dwivedi, O. P., & Jabbra, J. G. (1988). Public service responsibility and accountability. In: O. Dwivedi & J. Jabbra (Eds), *Public service accountability: A comparative perspective* (pp. 1–16). West Hartford, CT: Kumarian Press.

Elling, R. C. (1992). *Public management in the states: A comparative study of administrative performance and politics*. Westport, CT: Praeger.

Epstein, P. (1992). Measuring the performance of public services. In: M. Holzer (Ed.), *Productivity handbook* (pp. 161–193). New York: Marcel Dekker.

Epstein, P. (1996). Redeeming the promise of performance measurement: Issues and obstacles for governments in the United States. In: A. Halachmi & G. Bouckaert (Eds.), *Organizational performance and measurement in the public sector: Toward service, effort and accomplishment reporting* (pp. 51–76). Westport, CN: Quorum Books.

Ervin, O. L. (1980). The functions of budgeting: An elaboration of the Schick typology. *Midwest Review of Public Administration, 14*, 119–129.

Fenno, R. (1966). *The power of the purse*. Boston: Little, Brown & Co.

Finer, H. (1941). Administrative responsibility in a democratic government. *Public Administration Review, 1*, 335–350.

Florida Office of Program Policy Analysis and Government Accountability. (1997). *Performance-based program budgeting in Context: History and Comparison* (Report No. 86–77B). Tallahassee, FL: OPPAGA Report Production.

Forsythe, D. W. (1993). Financial management and the reinvention of government. *Public Productivity & Management Review, 16*(4), 415–423.

Franklin, A. (1999). Managing for results in Arizona: A fifth-year report card. *Public Productivity & Management Review, 23*(2), 194–209.

Franklin, A., Cawley, M., & O'Sullivan-Katchel, P. (1998). Renovations and innovations in program evaluation: The Arizona experience and its potential for more widespread applicability. *Public Productivity & Management Review, 22*(1), 88–106.

Frederickson, H. G. (1992). Painting bull's-eyes around bullet holes. *Governing, 6*(1).

Frederickson, H. G. (1996). Comparing the reinventing government movement with the new public administration. *Public Administration Review, 56*, 263–269.

Friedrich, C. J. (1940). Public policy and the nature of administrative responsibility. In: E. Mason & C. Friedrich (Eds.), *Public Policy 1940* (pp. 3–24). Cambridge: Harvard University Press.

Garvey, G. J., & DiIulio, J. J. (1994). Sources of public service overregulation. In: J. DiIulio (Ed.), *Deregulating the public service: Can government be improved* (pp. 12–36). Washington, D.C.: The Brookings Institution.

Goodsell, C. T. (1983). *The case for bureaucracy: a public administration polemic.* Chatham, N.J.: Chatham House Publishers.

Goodsell, C. T. (1993). Reivent government or rediscover it? *Public Administration Review, 53*, 85–87.

Governmental Accounting Standards Board. (1990). *Service efforts and accomplishments reporting: Its time has come.* Norwalk, CT: Governmental Accounting Standards Board.

Governmental Accounting Standards Board. (1992). *Preliminary views on concepts related to service efforts and accomplishments reporting: Its time has come.* Norwalk, CT: Governmental Accounting Standards Board.

Governmental Accounting Standards Board. (1994). *Concepts statement no. 2: Service efforts and accomplishments reporting.* Norwalk, CT: Governmental Accounting Standards Board.

Gray, A., & Jenkins, B. (1993). Horses to the water: Budgeting, auditing, and evaluation in seven governments. In: A. Gray, B. Jenkins & B. Segsworth (Eds.), *Budgeting, auditing, and evaluation: Functions and integration in seven governments* (pp. 185–208). London: Transaction Publishers.

Gray, A., Jenkins, B., & Segsworth, B. (Eds.) (1993). *Budgeting auditing and evaluation: Functions and integration in seven governments.* London: Transaction Publishers.

Greathouse, F. L., & Funkhouser, M. (1988). Audit standards and performance auditing in state government. *The Government Accountants Journal, 36*(4), 56–60.

Greiner, J. (1996). Positioning performance measurement for the twenty-first century. In: A. Halachmi & G. Bouckaert (Eds), *Organizational performance and measurement in the public sector: Toward service, effort and accomplishment reporting* (pp. 11–50). Westport, CN: Quorum Books.

Grifel, S. S. (1993). Performance measurement and budgetary decision making. *Public Productivity & Management Review, 16*(4), 402–407.

Grizzle, G. A. (1986). Does budget format really govern the actions of budget makers?. *Public Budgeting & Finance, 6*, pp. 60–69.

Hackbart, M. M., & Carson, R. J. (1993). Budget theory and state budget practice: Analysis and perspective. *Public Budgeting & Financial Management, 5*(1), 115–130.

Halachmi, A. (1996). Promises and possible pitfalls on the way to SEA reporting. In: A. Halachmi & G. Bouckaert (Eds), *Organizational performance and measurement in the public sector: Toward service, effort and accomplishment reporting* (pp. 77–100). Westport, CN: Quorum Books.

Hale, S., & Hyde, A. C. (1994). Reengineering in the public sector. *Public Productivity & Management Review, 18*(2), pp. 127–132.

Harris, J. (1995). Service efforts and accomplishments standards: Fundamental questions of an emerging concept. *Public Budgeting and Finance, 15*(4),18–37.

Hatry, H. P. (1989). Determining the effectiveness of government services. In: J. L. Perry (Ed.), *Handbook of Public Administration* (pp. 469–482). San Francisco: Jossey-Bass.

Hatry, H. P. (1999). Mini-symposium on intergovernmental comparative performance data. *Public Administration Review, 59*(2), 101–104.

Hatry, H. P., Blair, L. H., Fisk, D. M., Greiner, J. M., Hall, J. R., & Schaenman, P. S. (1992). *How effective are your community services?* (2nd ed.). Washington, D.C.: The Urban Institute.

Heeks, R. (Ed.). (1999). *Reinventing government in the information age: International practice in IT-enabled public sector reform.* London: Routledge.

Hendrick, R. (1996, October). *Fulfilling the promise of performance measurement in local government: Caveats and complications.* Paper presented at the Annual Conference of the Asssociation of Public Budgeting and Financial Management, Washington, D.C.

Horner, C. (1994). Deregulating the federal service: Is the time right? In: J. DiIulio (Ed.), *Deregulating the public service: Can government be improved*? (pp. 85–101). Washington, D.C.: The Brookings Institution.

Howard, S. K. (1973). *Changing state budgeting*. Lexington, KY: Council of State Governments.

International City/County Management Association (ICMA). (1999). *Comparative performance measurement: FY 1997 data report.* Washington, D.C.: ICMA.

Ingraham, P. W., & Romzek, B. S. (1994). Introduction: Issues raised by current reform efforts. In: P. Ingraham & B. Romzek (Eds.), *New paradigms for government* (pp. 1–14). San Francisco, CA: Jossey-Bass Publishers.

Jones, L. R. (1993). Counterpoint essay: Nine reasons why the CFO Act may not achieve its objectives. *Public Budgeting & Finance, 13*(1), 87–94.

Jones, L. R., & McCaffery, J. L. (1993). Implementation of the federal Chief Financial Officers Act. *Public Budgeting & Finance, 15*(1), 68–76.

Jones, L. R., & Thompson, F. (1993). Reform of budget execution control. *Public Budgeting & Finance, 13*(1), 33–49.

Jones, R. (1994). An indictment of performance measurement in the public sector. In: E. Buschor & K. Schedler (Eds), *Perspectives on performance measurement and public sector accounting* (pp. 43–57). Berne: Haupt.

Jordan, M. M., & Hackbart, M. M. (1999). Performance Budgeting and performance funding in the states: A status assessment. *Public Budgeting & Finance, 19*(1), 68–88.

Joyce, P. G. (1993a). The reiterative nature of budget reform: is there anything new in federal budgeting. *Public Budgeting & Finance, 13*(3), 36–48.

Joyce, P. G. (1993b). Using performance measures for federal budgeting: Proposals and prospects. *Public Budgeting and Financial Management 5*, pp. 3–17.

Joyce P. G. (1996a). Jesse Burkhead and the multiple uses of federal budgets: A contemporary perspective. *Public Budgeting & Finance, 16*(2), 59–78.

Joyce, P. G. (1996b). *Using performance information in the federal budget process: Where do we stand and where are we headed*? Paper presented at the Annual Conference of the Association for Public Budgeting and Financial Management, Washington, D. C.

Kaufman, H. (1977). *Red tape: Its origins, uses, and abuses*. Washington, D.C.: The Brookings Institution.

Kaufman, H. (1996). Music of the squares: A lifetime of study of public administration. *Public Administration Review, 56*, 127–138.

Kettl, D. F. (1994). Managing on the frontiers of knowledge: The learning organization. In: P. Ingraham & B. Romzek (Eds), *New paradigms for government* (pp. 19–40). San Francisco, CA: Jossey-Bass Publishers.

Kettl, D. F. (2000). Public administration at the millennium: The state of the field. *Journal of Public Administration Research and Theory, 10*(1), 7–34.

Key, V. O. (1940). The lack of a budget theory. *American Political Science Review, 34*, pp. 1137–40.

Khademian, A. M. (1995). The new dynamic of legislating and the implications for delegation: What's to be expected on the receiving end. *Journal of Public Administration Research and Theory, 5*(1), 19–44.

King, L. (1996, July). Office of Planning & Budget, Utah's budget process and use of performance measures. Unpublished survey data.

Klay, W. E. (1992). Revenue forecasting: A learning perspective. In: J. Rabin (Ed.), *Handbook of comparative budgeting*. New York: Marcel Decker.

Kopczynki, M., & Lombardo, M. (1999). Comparative performance measurement: Insights and lessons learned for a consortium effort. *Public Administration Review, 59*(2), 124–134.

Lan, Z., & Rainey, H. (1992). Goals, rules, and effectiveness in public, private, and hybrid organizations: More evidence on frequent assertions about differences. *Journal of Public Administration and Theory, 2*, 5–24.

Landau, M., & Stout, R. (1979). To manage is not to control: Or the folly of type II errors. *Public Administration Review, 39*(2), 148–155.

Lauth, T. P. (1979). Zero-base budgeting in Georgia state government: Myth and reality. *Public Administration Review, 38*, 420–428.

Lee, R. D. Jr. (1991). Developments in state budgeting: Trends of two decades. *Public Administration Review, 51*(3), 254–261.

Lee, R. D. Jr. (1992). The use of executive guidance in state budget preparation. *Public Budgeting & Finance, 13*(3), 19–31.

Lee, R. D. Jr. (1997). A quarter century of state budgeting practices. *Public Administration Review, 57*(2), 133–140.

Lee, R. D. Jr., & Burns, R. C. (2000). Performance measurement in state budgeting: Advancement and backsliding from 1990 to 1995. *Public Budgeting & Finance, 20*(1), 38–54.

Lee, R. D. Jr., & Johnson, R. W. (1989). *Public budgeting systems* (4th ed.). Rockville, MD: Aspen Publication.

Leithe, J. L. (1997). *Implementing performance measurement in government: Illustrations and resources*. Chicago, IL: Government Finance Officers Association.

LeLoup, L. T. (1988). From microbudgeting to macrobudgeting: Evolution in theory and practice. In: I. Rubin (Ed.), *New directions in budget theory* (pp. 19–42). Albany, NY: State University of New York Press.

Leonard, B., Cook, J., & McNeil, J. (1995). The role of budget and financial reform in making government work better and cost less. *Public Budgeting & Finance, 15*(1), 4–17.

Levine, C. H. & Rubin, I. S. (Eds). (1980). *Fiscal stress and public policy*. Beverly Hills, CA: Sage Publications.

Lewis, C. (2000). Efficiently taking soundings in a sea of change: Two histories of public budgeting and finance. Public Administration Review, *60*(2), 183–185.

Lewis, V. B. (1952). Toward a theory of budgeting. Public *Administration Review, 12*, 42–54.

Lewis, W. (Ed.). (1968). *Budget concepts for economic analysis*. Washington, D.C.: Brookings Institution.

Light, P. C. (1993). *Monitoring government: Inspectors General and the search for accountability*. Washington, D.C.: The Brookings Institution.

Louisiana Office of Planning & Budget. (1996, January). *Manageware: A practical guide to managing for results*. Baton Rouge, LA: State Printing Office.

Lowi, T. J. (1993). Legitimizing public administration: A disturbed dissent. *Public Administration Review, 53*, 261–263.

Lynch, T. D. (1990). *Public budgeting in America* (3rd. ed.). Englewood Cliffs, NJ: Prentice Hall.

Mansfield, H. C. (1982). Accountability and congressional oversight. In: B. Smith & J. Carroll (Eds.), *Improving the accountability and performance of government* (pp. 61–70). Washington, D.C.: The Brookings Institution.

Marlowe, H. A., & Arrington, L. W. (1994). The *re-ing* of local government: Understanding and shaping governmental change. *Public Productivity & Management Review, 17*, 299–311.

McIntyre, J. T. (1980). Discretionary control of the federal budget. In: W. S. Moore & R. G. Penner (Eds). *The constitution and the budget: Are constitutional limits on tax, spending, and budget powers desirable at the federal level?* (pp. 57–62). Washington, D.C.: American Enterprise Institute.

Melkers, J., & Willoughby, K. (1998). The state of the states: Performance-based budgeting requirements in 47 out of 50. *Public Administration Review, 58*(1), 66–73.

Miller, G. (1992). Productivity and the budget process. In: M. Holzer (Ed.), *Public Productivity Handbook* (pp. 227–252). New York: Marcel Dekker.

Minnesota, Department of Finance (1996, August). *1996 Performance report instructions*. St. Paul: State of Minnesota.

Minnesota, Office of the Legislative Auditor. (1994, February). *Performance budgeting*. St. Paul, Minnesota: State of Minnesota.

Moe, R. C. (1994). The "reinventing government" exercise: Misinterpreting the problem, misjudging the consequences. *Public Administration Review, 54*, 111–122.

Moe, R. C., & Gilmour, R. S. (1995). Rediscovering principles of public administration: The neglected foundation of public law. *Public Administration Review, 55*, 135–146.

Monitor Publishing. (1996). *State yellow book*. New York: Monitor Publishing Company.

Moon, J. J. (1999). The pursuit of managerial entrepreneurship: Does organization matter? *Public Administration Review, 59*(1), 31–43.

Mosher, F. C. (1982). Comment on accountability and congressional oversight. In: B. Smith & J. Carroll (Eds.), *Improving the accountability and performance of government* (pp. 71–74). Washington, D.C.: The Brookings Institution.

Mosso, D. (1999). Accounting for the business of government – new goals, old myths. *Public Budgeting & Finance, 19*(4) 65–74.

National Academy of Public Administration. (1983, November). *Revitalizing federal management: Managers and their overburdened systems*. Washington, D. D : National Academy of Public Administration.

National Association of State Budget Officers. (1987, July). *Budgetary processes in the states*. Washington, D.C.: National Association of State Budget Officers.

National Association of State Budget Officers. (1990, October). *The use of performance measures by the states*. Report prepared for the Performance Measures Special Study Group at the meeting of the National Association of State Budget Officers, Boulder, CO.

National Association of State Budget Officers. (1992, July). *Budget processes in the states*. Washington, D.C.: National Association of State Budget Officers.

National Association of State Budget Officers. (1995). *Budget processes in the states*. Washington, D.C.: National Association of State Budget Officers.

National Association of State Budget Officers. (1996, April). *Restructuring and innovations in state management*. Washington, D.C.: National Association of State Budget Officers.

National Association of State Budget Officers. (1997. *Budget processes in the states*. Washington, D.C.: National Association of State Budget Officers.

National Commission on the State and Local Public Service. (1993). Hard truths/tough choices: An agenda for state and local reform. In: F. Thompson (Ed.), *Revitalizing state and local public service: Strengthening performance, accountability, and citizen confidence* (pp. 332–403). San Francisco: Jossey-Bass.

National Conference of State Legislatures. (1994). *The performance budget revisited: A report on state budget reform*. (Legislative Finance Papers. No 91). Denver, CO.: Fiscal Affairs Program.

National Commission on the State and Local Public Service. (1995). *Paths to performance: A seven state focus*. New York: The Nelson A. Rockefeller Institute of Government.

National Performance Review. (1993a). *From red tape to results: Creating a government that works better and costs less*. Washington, D.C.: U.S. Government Printing Office.

National Performance Review. (1993b). *Mission-driven, results-oriented budgeting: Accompanying report of the National Performance Review*. Washington, D.C.: U.S. Government Printing Office.

National Performance Review. (1993c). *Streamlining management control: Accompanying report of the National Performance Review*. Washington, D.C.: U.S. Government Printing Office.

National Performance Review. (1997, June). *Serving the American public: Best practices in performance measurement*. [on-line]. Available: http://www.npr.gov/library/papers/benchmrk/nprbook.html.

Normanton, E. L. (1971). Public accountability and audit: A reconnaissance. In: B. Smith & D. Hague (Eds.), *The dilemma of accountability in modern government: Independence versus control*, pp. 311–378. New York: St. Martin's Press.

O'Loughlin, M. G. (1990). What is bureaucratic accountability and how can we measure it? *Administration & Society*, *22*(3), 275–302.

Organization For Economic Cooperation and Development (OECD). (1994). *Performance management in government: Performance measurement and results oriented management*. Paris: OECD.

Organization For Economic Cooperation and Development (OECD). (1995). *Budgeting for results: Perspectives on public expenditure management*. Paris: OECD.

Organization For Economic Cooperation and Development (OECD). (1997). *Modern budgeting*. Paris: OECD.

Osborne, D., & Gaebler, R. (1992). *Reinventing government: How the entrepreneurial spirit is transforming the public sector*. Reading, MA: Addison-Wesley.

Peters, B. G., & Savoie, D. J. (1996). Managing incoherence: The coordination and empowerment conundrum. *Public Administration Review, 56*(3), 281–289.

Pilegge, J. C. (1992). Budget reforms. In: J. Rabin (Ed.), *Public Productivity Handbook* (pp. 195–212). New York: Marcel Dekker.

Poister, T. H., Hatry, H. P., Fisk, D. M., & Griener, J. M. (1985). Centralized productivity improvement efforts in state government. *Public Productivity Review, 9*(1), 5–24.

Poister, T. H., & Streib, G. (1989). Management tools in municipal government: Trends over the past decade. *Public Administration Review, 49*, 240–248.

Poister, T. H., & Streib, G. (1995). MBO in municipal government: Variations of a traditional management tool. Public Administration Review. *Public Administration Review, 55*, 48–56.

Poister, T. H., & Streib, G. (1999). Performance measurement in municipal government: Assessing the state of the practice. *Public Administration Review, 59*(4), 325–336.

Popovich, M. G. (Ed.). (1998). *Creating high-performance government organizations: A practical guide for public managers*. San Francisco: Jossey-Bass.

Premchand, A. (1998). Umbrella themes obscure real problems: An appraisal of recent efforts to improve financial management. *Public Budgeting & Finance, 18*(3), 72–88.

Pyhrr, P. A. (1977). The zero-base approach to government budgeting. *Public Administration Review, 37*, 15–41.

Radin, B. A. (2000). The Government Performance and Results Act and the tradition of federal management reform: Square pegs in round holes? *Journal of Public Administration Research and Theory, 10*(1), 111–135.

Rainey, H. G., Pandey, S., & Bozeman, B. (1995). Research note: Public and private managers' perceptions of red tape. *Public Administration Review, 55*, 568–574.

Reading, M. (July, 1996). Telephone interview with budget officer for performance measures, Division of Budget & Planning, Office of Administration, State of Missouri.

Roberts, A. (1997). Performance-based organizations: Assessing the Gore plan. *Public Administration Review, 57*(6), 465–478.

Roberts, N. (2000). The synoptic model of strategic planning and the GPRA: Lacking a good fit with the political context. *Public productivity and Management Review, 23*(3), 297–311.

Romzek, B. S., & Dubnick, M. J. (1987). Accountability in the public sector: Lessons from the Challenger tragedy. *Public Administration Review, 47*, 227–238.

Romzek, B. S., & Dubnick, M. J. (1993). Accountability and expectations in American public administration. In: J. Perry (Ed.), *Research in public administration* (pp. 37–78). Greenwich, CN: JAI Press .

Romzek, B. S., & Dubnick, M. J. (1994). Issues of accountability in flexible personnel systems. In: P. Ingraham & B. Romzek (Eds.), *New paradigms for government* (pp. 263–294). San Francisco, CA: Jossey-Bass Publishers.

Rose, R. (1977). Implementation and evaporation: The record of MBO. *Public Administration Review, 37*, 64–71.

Rosen, E. D. (1993). *Improving public sector productivity*. Newbury Park, CA: SAGE.

Rosenbloom, D. H. (1983). Public administration theory and the separation of powers. *Public Administration Review, 43*, 219–227.

Rosenbloom, D. H. (1993). Have an administrative Rx? Don't forget the politics! *Public Administration Review, 53*, 503–507.

Rosenbloom, D. H., & Ross, B. H. (1994). Administrative theory, political power, and government reform. In: P. Ingraham & B. Romzek (Eds.), *New paradigms for government* (pp. 145–167). San Francisco, CA: Jossey-Bass Publishers.

Rosenfeld, R. A. (1984). An expansion and application of Kaufman's model of red tape: The case of community development block grants. *Western Political Quarterly, 7*, 603–620.

Rubin, I. S. (Ed.). (1988). *New directions in budget theory*. Albany, New York: State University of New York Press.

Rubin, I. S. (1990). Budget theory and budget practice: How good the fit? *Public Administration Review, 40*, 179–189.

Rubin, I. S. (1992). Budgeting: Theory, concepts, methods, and issues. In: J. Rabin (Ed.), *Handbook of Public Budgeting* (pp. 3–22). New York: Marcel Dekker.

Rubin, I. S. (1993). *The politics of public budgeting: Getting and spending, borrowing and balancing* (2nd ed.). Chatham, NJ: Chatham House.

Rubin, I. S. (1995). Forum – Balanced budget world: Assessing the forum & realities. *The Public Manager, 24*(4), 23–25.

Saleh, H. A. (1991). Agency budget success in state legislatures: A comparative analysis. (Doctoral Dissertation, Florida State University) *Dissertation Abstracts International*, 52, 3427A.

Sandberg, B. (1996). Annual performance accounting and auditing: Is it possible? In: A. Halachmi & G. Bouckaert (Eds.), *Organizational performance and measurement in the public sector: Toward service, effort and accomplishment reporting* (pp. 167–186). Westport, CN: Quorum Books.

Schick, A. (1966). The road to PPB: The stages of budget reform. *Public Administration Review, 26*, 243–258.

Schick, A. (1973). A death in the bureaucracy: The demise of federal PPB. *Public Administration Review, 33*, 146–156.

Schick, A. (1977). Zero-base budgeting and sunset: Redundancy or symbiosis? *The Bureaucrat, 6*, 12–32.

Schick, A. (1979). *The status of zero-base budgeting in the states*. Washington, D.C.: National Association of State Budget Officers.

Schick, A. (1980). Budgeting as an administrative process. In. A. Schick (Ed.). *Perspectives on budgeting* (pp. 1–14). Washington, D.C.: American Society for Public Administration.

Schick, A. (1988). An inquiry into the possibility of a budgetary theory. In: I. S. Rubin (Ed.), *New directions in budget theory* (pp. 59–69). Albany: State University of New York.

Schick, A. (1990). Budgeting for results: Recent developments in five industrialized countries. *Public Administration Review, 50*, 26–34.

Schick, A. (1994a). From the old politics of budgeting to the new. *Public Budgeting & Finance, 14*(1), 135–144.

Schick, A. (1994b). Why study microbudgeting? In: J. Cogan, T. Muris & A. Schick (Eds.), *The Budget Puzzle: Understanding federal spending*. Stanford, CA: Stanford University Press.

Smith, B. L., & Hague, D. C. (Eds.). (1971). *The dilemma of accountability in modern government: Independence versus control*. New York: St. Martin's Press.

Smith, J. F. (1999). The benefits and threats of PBB: An assessment of modern reform. *Public Budgeting & Finance, 19*(3), 3–15.

Sorensen, R. J. (1994). Improving government allocation: The impact of alternative budgetary methods. *International Review of Administrative Sciences, 60*, 5–11.

Stanford, K. A. (1990). State legislative appropriation committees: An exploration of factors that may influence the orientation of their deliberations (Doctoral Dissertation, Florida State University, 1989). *Dissertation Abstracts International*, 50, 3427A.

Stanford, K. A. (1992). State budget deliberations: Do legislators have a strategy?. *Public Administration Review, 52*, pp. 16–25.

Straussman, J. D. (1979). A typology of budgetary environments: Notes on the prospects for reform. *Administration & Society, 11*(2), 216–226.

Straussman, J. D. (1986). Courts and public purse strings: Have portraits of budgeting missed something? *Public Administration Review, 46*, 345–351.

Straussman, J. D. (1988). Rights-based budgeting. In: I. S. Rubin (Ed.), *New directions in budget theory* (pp. 100–123). Albany, NY: State University of New York Press.

Thompson, J. A. (1987). Agency requests, gubernatorial support, and budget success in state legislatures revisited. *Journal of Politics, 49*, 756–779.

Thompson, F. J. (1993). The challenges revisited. In: F. Thompson (Ed.), *Revitalizing state and local public service: Strengthening performance, accountability, and citizen confidence* (pp. 309–327). San Francisco: Jossey-Bass.

Thompson, F. (1994). Mission-driven, result-oriented budgeting: Fiscal administration and the new public management. *Public Budgeting & Finance, 14*(3), 90–105.

Thompson, J. R. (2000). The dual potentialities of performance measurement: The case of the Social Security Administration. *Public Productivity and Management Review, 23*(3), 267–281.

U.S. Congressional Budget Office. (1993, July). *Using performance measures in the federal budget process*. Washington, D.C.: Government Printing Office.

U.S. General Accounting Office. (1993, February). *Performance budgeting state experiences and implications for the federal government*. Prepared by the

Accounting and Financial Management Division. Washington, D.C.: Government Printing Office.

U.S. General Accounting Office. (1994, September). *Budget object classification: Origin and recent trends.* Prepared by the Accounting and Financial Management Division. Washington, D.C.: Government Printing Office.

U.S. General Accounting Office. (1997, March). *Performance budgeting: Past initiatives offer insights for GPRA implementation.* Washington, D.C.: Government Printing Office.

U.S. Office of Management and Budget. (1994, August). *Preparation and Submission of Budget Estimates.* Washington, D.C.: Government Printing Office.

Van Daniker, R. P. (1994). Performance measurement in the states. In: E. Buschor & K. Schedler (Eds.), *Perspectives on performance measurement and public sector accounting* (pp. 43–57). Berne: Haupt.

Virginia Department of Planning & Budget. (1995, August). Instructions for setting strategic goals and submitting decision packages: Goal setting and performance budgeting for the 1996–98 biennium. Richmond: State of Virginia.

Wallach, H. C. (1977). Center for census use studies: Small area data technology. In: K. Finsterbusch & C. P. Wolf (Eds.), *Methodology of social impact assessment.* Stroudsburg, PA: Dowden, Hutchinson and Ross.

Warfel, D. (July, 1996). Telephone interview with Budget Officer, Office of the Budget, State of Pennsylvania.

Wheat, E. M. (1991). The activist auditor: A new player in state and local politics. *Public Administration Review, 51*, 385–292.

Whicker, M. L. (1992). Toward a grander budget theory. *Public Administration Review, 52*, 601–603.

White, J. (1994). (Almost) nothing new under the sun: Why the work of budgeting remains incremental. *Public Budgeting & Finance, 14*(1), 113–133.

Wholey, J. S. (1999). Performance-based management: Responding to the challenges. *Public Productivity and Management Review*, 22(3), 288–307.

Wholey, J. S. & Hatry, H. P. (1992). The case for performance monitoring. *Public Administration Review, 6*, 604–610.

Wildavsky, A. (1964). *The politics of the budgetary process.* Boston: Little, Brown.

Wildavsky, A. (1980). Political implications of budgetary reform. In: A. Schick (Ed.), *Perspectives on budgeting* (pp. 70–80). Washington, D.C.: American Society for Public Administration.

Wildavsky, A. (1986). *Budgeting: A comparative theory of budgetary processes* (2nd. ed.). New Brunswick, NJ: Transaction Books.

Wildavsky, A. (1992a). Political implications of budget reform: A retrospective. *Public Administration Review, 52*, 594–599.

Wildavsky, A. (1992b). *The new politics of the budgetary process.* Glenview, IL: Scott Foresman).

Willoughby, K. G. (1992). Decision making orientations of state government budget analysts: Rationalists or incrementalists? *Public Budgeting & Financial Management*, *3*(1), 67–114.

Willoughby, K. G., & Melkers, J. E. (2000). Implementing PBB: Conflicting views of success. *Public Budgeting & Finance*, *20*(1), 105–120.

Wilson, J. Q. (1989). *Bureaucracy: What government agencies do and why they do it.* New York: Basic Books.

Wilson, J. Q. (1994). Can the bureaucracy be deregulated? Lessons from government agencies (pp. 37–61). In: J. DiIulio (Ed.), *Deregulating the public service: Can government be improved?*. Washington, D.C.: The Brookings Institution.

Wilson, L. A., & Sylvia, R. (1993). Changing revenue conditions and state budgetary decisions. *Journal of Public administration Research and Theory*, *3*(3), 319–333.

Wisconsin Commission for the study of administrative value and efficiency. (1995, January). *Citizen, community, government: Wisconsin: The 21st Century.* Madison, WI: State of Wisconsin.

APPENDIX A: BUDGET PROCESSES AND USE OF PERFORMANCE MEASURES: QUESTIONNAIRE

In [STATE NAME]:

1. There is an identifiable ongoing program or formal initiative charged with the task of integrating performance measures including inputs, outputs, and outcomes into the state's budget process.

Yes___ No___

2. This initiative is coordinated by a unit located in the central administration or reporting to the governor or other official of the central administration.

Yes___ No___

3. The integration of performance measurement data into the state budget process is extended to select if not all operating agencies in a uniform manner.

Yes___ No___

I. Performance measurement information

1. Performances measurement information is used in the budget process and must be reported by:

All agencies\programs ___
Select agencies\programs___
Not apply___

2. If only select agencies/programs, which ones were required to submit performance measurement data for FY 97 (please list).

____

____

____

3. Performance measures are reported at the following level(s):

Agency ___
Program___
Subprogram___

Other___
Not Apply ___

4. Performance measurement data are required for:

All funds ___
State general funds ___
Other (please list)_____
Not apply ___

5. Performance measures are linked to broader strategic planning initiatives which identify missions and goals:

Statewide mission/goals ___
Agency mission/goals___
Program mission/goals___
Not apply ___

6. Performance reporting legislation/executive order/administrative rule was passed in:

Year ________

7. Agencies/programs were first required to submit performance measurement data with their budget request in fiscal year:____ (If select agencies/ programs phased in please note).

____
____
____

8. Performance measures are published in:

Budget Document ___
Budget Supplement ___
Separate Performance Report___
Not published___

9. Number of years performance measures cover:

Years ___
Not apply ___

10. Performance measures are monitored:

Biennially___
Annually___
Quarterly___
Other (please list) ___
Not Apply___

11. Performance measures are monitored by:

Agency_____
Exec. Central Budget Staff _____
Legislative Central Budget Staff____

State Auditor____
Other (please list)____
Not Apply____

12. Types of performance measurement information reported by agency/ program for use in annual/biennial budget process:
input: resources expended (e.g. dollars, personnel)____
output: the quantity of products or units of service provided ____
outcome: the results and quality of service delivered ___
efficiency: the cost, in dollars or employee hours, per unit of output or outcome ___

13. Standards against which agency/program performance is compared:
Previous performance ____
Pre-set targets ____
Similar organizations ___
Best organizations (i.e. benchmarking) ___
Other (please list) ____

14. Current use(s) of performance measures in budget process is(are) [please rank 1–4 (1 being the primary use] or Not Apply (NA)
Informational ___
Budgetary decision making ___
Audit ___
Periodic review to retain, eliminate, or modify agency/program ____
Other (please list)___

15. Performance measurement data are verified by:
Central executive budget staff ___
Central legislative budget staff____
State auditor___
Other ____
Not Apply ___

16. The integration of budgeting, accounting and performance information systems:
Is available in a centralized management information system___
Is under development as a centralized management information system at the present time ___
Is being developed by individual agencies ___
Has not yet been addressed ___

17. Additional funds for management information systems have been appropriated to implement performance measurement initiatives in the budget process.
FY 97 Yes ___

FY 97 No ___
Prior fiscal years Yes ___
Prior fiscal years No ___

18. Additional funds (excluding management information systems) have been appropriated to central budget offices to implement performance measurement initiatives in the budget process.

FY 97 Yes ___
FY 97 No ___
Prior fiscal years Yes ___
Prior fiscal years No ___

19. Additional funds (excluding management information systems) have been appropriated to agencies/programs to implement performance measurement initiatives in the budget process.

FY 97 Yes ___
FY 97 No ___
Prior fiscal years Yes ___
Prior fiscal years No ___

20. Training is (has been) conducted for central executive budget staff on performance measurement and monitoring:

Yes, in 1996 ___
Yes for the past ___years
No ___

21. Training is (has been) conducted for central legislative budget staff on performance measurement and monitoring:

Yes, in 1996 ___
Yes for the past ___years
No ___

22. Training is (has been) conducted at the agency/program level on performance measurement and monitoring:

Yes, in 1996 ___
Yes for the past ___years
No ___

II. Budget Process (Please note if process differs for pilot or select agencies undertaking performance budget reform)

1. Budget cycle

Biennial ___
Annual___
Other ___

2. In budget preparation are agencies/programs given spending targets by central staff

Yes___
No ___
3. Approaches used in annual/biennial budget process
Incremental, line item ___
Program budgeting ___
Zero Based Budgeting ___
Other ___
4. Budget format of agency requests:
Line item ___
Organizational unit ___
Program ___
Lump sum___
5. Budget format of executive budget submitted to legislature
Line item ___
Organizational unit ___
Program ___
Lump sum ___
6. Budget format of appropriation bill
Line item ___
Organizational unit ___
Program ___
Lump sum ___
7. Budget format of accounting records
Line item ___
Organizational unit ___
Program ___
Lump sum ___
8. Officials authorized to transfer (non emergency) appropriations between programs in separate departments/agencies
Not allowed ___
Legislature ____
Governor ___
Executive Budget Agency___
Agency ___
Other ___
9. Officials authorized to transfer (non emergency) appropriations between programs within the same department/agency
Not allowed ___
Legislature ____
Governor ___

Executive Budget Agency___
Agency ___
Other ___

10. Officials authorized to transfer (non emergency) appropriations between object classes within a program or budget unit

Not allowed ___
Legislature ____
Governor ___
Executive Budget Agency___
Agency ___
Other ___

11. Allotments apply to:

All agencies ___
All funds ___
Select agencies ___
Select funds ___
Not apply ____

12. Frequency of allotment requests

Annual ____
Semiannual____
Quarterly ___
Monthly ____
As requested ____
Other ____
Not apply ____

13. Are annual/biennial costs of federal mandates to the state estimated?

Yes, by the central executive budget office ___
Yes, by agencies/programs ___
Yes, by other department/office ___
Yes, but are not regularly estimated every budget cycle by any office/program ___
No, costs of mandates are not estimated ___

14. Additional comments regarding state's budget process and use of performance measurement data:

APPENDIX B: PRACTITIONERS' PERCEPTIONS ON ACCOUNTABILITY, DISCRETION, AND PERFORMANCE BUDGET REFORM: QUESTIONNAIRE

September 6, 1996

«fname» «lname», «jobtitle»
«address1»
«address2»
«address3»
«address4»
«city», «state» «zip»

Dear «prefix» «lname»:

Today, the public and its elected leaders want government to do more with less and to better serve the citizen/taxpayer while doing it. Much attention has been paid to the need for change in budgeting from a focus on process to results. There also have been many prescriptions put forth as to how this change should come about. Less attention has been directed toward practitioners' views on their budget process and their assessment of the expectations for its reform. As the top administrator of the Department of «area», I would like to know your views on the budget process in «state» and on alternative constraints or accountability claims (i.e. fiscal, legal, bureaucratic, and political) that may affect administrative discretion in making budget decisions.

The enclosed questionnaire is being sent to top administrators like yourself, and to the central budget staff that review this program area in all fifty states. While this survey includes questions examining changes brought about by the implementation of performance budget reform, participating in this survey does not require that your department use performance measures and standards in your annual/biennial budget process. A separate review, examining each state's use of performance measures and the stage of development in adopting performance budget reform has been conducted. It is, therefore, understood that the use of performance measures in budgeting may be at varying stages of development or not used at all. Of interest to me, is whether the perceptions of practitioners regarding the enclosed questions change with the advancement of reform. If you are interested in the responses from practitioners in other states, a summary of the findings will be sent to you, just note that you would like to be sent a copy in the space provided at the end of the questionnaire.

Appreciating the many demands on your time, the questionnaire is short and takes approximately 15 minutes to complete. A self-addressed postpaid envelope is enclosed for your convenience. Your participation in

this project is voluntary. Return of the questionnaire will be considered your consent to participate. The responses will be kept confidential and will not be reported in a way that identifies individual respondents or specific agencies/program areas in a state. If you have any questions, you can contact me at telephone number: (602) 863–3032 or via email: kathy.anders@asu.edu.

Please take some time now to respond to these questions. It is important that I receive your response within the next two weeks. After two weeks, if I have not received your response, I will contact you to answer any questions that you may have or to determine if you need an additional questionnaire. Thank you very much for your help. Your views are what will make this research project a success.

Sincerely,

Enclosure

Kathleen K. Anders

SURVEY OF STATE AGENCY ADMINISTRATORS

This questionnaire seeks your views on the state's current budget process and administrative discretion in budget decision making . Please answer the following questions based on your experience at the Dept. of [name]. The questions are grouped into seven sections which, except for general information, address alternative constraints or accountability claims (i.e. fiscal, legal, bureaucratic, and political) that may affect discretion in budget decisions. While the survey examines changes brought about by the implementation of performance budget reform, questions in Sections I through III do not require that your program area use performance measures and standards (e.g. outputs and outcomes) in your annual/biennial budget process. The responses from this nationwide survey will be confidential and will not be reported in a way that identifies individual respondents or specific agencies /program areas in a state. If you would like a summary of the results of this survey, please check the space provided at the end of the questionnaire. Recognizing the demands on your time, this questionnaire is short and takes approximately 15 minutes to complete.

Section I: Fiscal constraints *(Please circle the extent to which you agree or disagree with each of the following statements)*

Strongly Agree 1	2	Agree 3	4	Disagree 5	6	Strongly Disagree 7

1. The means of financing, (e.g. statutory dedications, user fees, interagency transfers, and/or federal funds) pose significant restrictions on the budget decisions administrators can make.	1	2	3	4	5	6	7
2. Compulsory adjustments common to all state agencies (e.g. merit pay, group insurance, etc.) significantly limit the flexibility administrators have in their programs' budget decisions.	1	2	3	4	5	6	7
3. In our agency, multiyear, automatic funding decisions (e.g. indexing for inflation, formula funding) significantly restrict our discretion in making budget decisions.	1	2	3	4	5	6	7
4. The dollars available for agencies'/programs' budget request s limit the ability of administrators to make spending decisions based on their own judgment and knowledge of program needs.	1	2	3	4	5	6	7
5. The dollars available for agencies'/programs' budget requests force administrators to use their expertise to make performance enhancing and budget saving decisions.	1	2	3	4	5	6	7

6. Overall, approximately what percentage of this agency's budget request in FY 97 do you perceive is discretionary, that is, not determined by multiyear, automatic funding decisions, mandates from other levels or branches of government, compulsory statewide adjustments, or ties to specific revenue sources? __________%

Section II: Legal constraints *(Please circle the extent to which you agree or disagree with each of the following statements)*

Strongly Agree		Agree		Disagree		Strongly Disagree
1	2	3	4	5	6	7

1. A program's enabling statutes significantly limit an administrator's discretion in making budget decisions.	1	2	3	4	5	6	7
2. Constitutional provisions, federal mandates, and/or court decrees significantly limit an administrator's ability to make spending decisions based on his or her knowledge of program needs.	1	2	3	4	5	6	7
3. Answerability to the law, will dominate how annual/biennial budget decisions are made regardless of what program outcomes or results are achieved.	1	2	3	4	5	6	7
4. A significant portion of the current fiscal year's operating budget for this agency is determined by constitutional provisions, federal mandates, and/or court decrees.	1	2	3	4	5	6	7

5. Approximately what percentage of the current fiscal year's operating budget for this agency is required to be spent in certain ways because of constitutional provisions, federal mandates, and/or court decrees? ____________%

Section III: Administrative discretion *(Please circle the extent to which you agree or disagree with each of the following statements)*

Strongly Agree		Agree		Disagree		Strongly Disagree
1	2	3	4	5	6	7

1. I think that the use of performance measures and standards in budgeting *will* bring about a performance oriented budget process that encourages entrepreneurial behavior by administrators in budgetary decision making.	1	2	3	4	5	6	7
2. I think that the use of performance measures and standards in budgeting *will* bring about a performance oriented budget process that grants administrators greater discretion in exercising their own judgment and professional expertise in budgetary decisions.	1	2	3	4	5	6	7
3. I think that the use of performance measures and standards in budgeting *will* change accountability in budgeting from compliance with rules to accountability for results.	1	2	3	4	5	6	7

4. How important do you think the following factors are in realizing a performance oriented budgeting process that would promote the ability of adminstrators to utilize their professional expertise and knowledge of program needs in budgetary decisions? *(Please circle the response that indicates the importance of the following factors in doing so)*

Section III: Administrative discrection (Continued)

Strongly Agree 1	2	Agree 3	4	Disagree 5	6	Strongly Disagree 7

Reduction of administrative rules, procedures, guidelines and reporting requirements in the budget process	1	2	3	4	5	6	7
Shift in political decision makers oversight focus from dollar inputs to program results	1	2	3	4	5	6	7
Change in the laws which restrict an administrator's ability to use his own discretion in budgetary decision making	1	2	3	4	5	6	7
A lessening of fiscal constraints, both in terms of more dollars available and more dollars available that are not restricted or tied to specific programs	1	2	3	4	5	6	7

Other *(please specify):*

____

____

Section IV: Administrative discretion & reform: *(Please circle the extent to which you agree or disagree with each of the following statements)*

Strongly Agree 1	2	Agree 3	4	Disagree 5	6	Strongly Disagree 7	Performance Measures Not Used 0

1. I have found that the use of performance measures and standards in budgeting *has* encouraged entrepreneurial behavior by administrators in budgetary decision making.	1	2	3	4	5	6	7	0
2. I have found that the use of performance measures and standards in budgeting *has* given administrators more discretion in exercising their own judgment and professional expertise in budgetary decisions.	1	2	3	4	5	6	7	0
3. I have found that the use of performance measures and standards in budgeting *has* changed accountability in budgeting from compliance with rules to accountability for results.	1	2	3	4	5	6	7	0
4. I think that our state is fairly advanced in integrating performance measures and standards into the budget process.	1	2	3	4	5	6	7	0

Section V: Bureaucratic Constraints *(Please circle the extent to which you agree or disagree with each of the following statements)*
The reporting of performance measures and standards (e.g. outputs and outcomes) in the budget process

Strongly Agree		Agree		Disagree		Strongly Disagree	Performance Measures Not Used
1	2	3	4	5	6	7	0

1. Increases the number of budget instructions and rules issued by the central budget office for use by agencies in preparing their budget requests.	1	2	3	4	5	6	7	0
2. Adds to, it does not replace, traditional line-item reporting requirements in agency budget requests.	1	2	3	4	5	6	7	0
3. Adds to, it does not replace, traditional line-item reporting requirements in the executive budget submitted to the legislature.	1	2	3	4	5	6	7	0
4. Has resulted in less itemization and detailed instructions in budget appropriations.	1	2	3	4	5	6	7	0
5. Reduces the number of budget rules, regulations and procedures agency administrators must comply with in the execution of their budget.	1	2	3	4	5	6	7	0
6. Increases the resources (time, people, and money) expended in complying with administrative rules, guidelines, procedures and reporting requirements in the annual/biennial budget process.	1	2	3	4	5	6	7	0
7. Requires that too much time, people and money be dedicated to administration of the annual/biennial budget process.	1	2	3	4	5	6	7	0
8. Overall, has little influence on political decision makers in determining an agency's/program's budget allocation.	1	2	3	4	5	6	7	0

Section VI. Political Constraints *(Please circle the extent to which you agree or disagree with each of the following statements)*

With the reporting of performance measures and standards (e.g. outputs and outcomes) in the budget process:

Strongly Agree		Agree		Disagree		Strongly Disagree	Performance Measures Not Used
1	2	3	4	5	6	7	0

1. There is a relaxation of control over agency transfers of funds during budget execution by delegating more authority to agencies or simplifying the procedures for getting transfers approved by higher authorities.	1	2	3	4	5	6	7	0
2. Agency administrators are granted more discretion in the timing or allotment of funds.	1	2	3	4	5	6	7	0
3. The legislature lessens spending controls and gives agency administrators more discretion in executing their budgets by using more flexible funding formats (e.g. lump sum appropriations).	1	2	3	4	5	6	7	0
4. The focus of political decision makers in budgeting shifts from program inputs or costs to the performance or outcomes of programs.	1	2	3	4	5	6	7	0
5. Control of legislators and central budget staff over agencies/programs in the budget process is strengthened.	1	2	3	4	5	6	7	0

6. Agency administrators may carry over to the next year (annual budgets) or to the next two years (biennial budgets) all or a portion of their end of year unobligated balances. *(Please check one)* _____ **Yes** _____ **No**

Section VII: General information *(Responses will be reported only in summary form. No individual respondents or specific agencies/program areas in a state will be identified.)*

Title ____________________________ **Years in current position** ________yrs.

Years in current organization ________yrs. **Years in state government** ________yrs.

What is the total operating budget of this agency for the current fiscal year?

$ ____________________

Currently, how many full time employees work for this agency? ________________

I would like to receive a summary of the results of this survey sent to the address below.

(Please check one) **No** _______ **Yes, in the mail** ______ **Yes, via email** ________

Name ________________________ **Address** ____________________________________

Phone (____)________________ ____________________________________

Email ________________________ ____________________________________

Please mail the questionnaire to me as soon as possible in the postage paid return envelope. It is important to the success of this project that I receive your responses within the next two weeks. Thank you very much for providing your views on these questions and taking the time to complete this questionnaire.

Kathy Anders
School of Public Affairs, Arizona State University
Return address for survey: 14035 N. Coral Gables Dr.
Phoenix, AZ 85023–6275
Email: kathy.anders@asu.edu Phone: (602) 863–3032

Printed and bound by CPI Group (UK) Ltd, Croydon, CR0 4YY
16/09/2026
14963401-0008